CW01334152

A Grand National Commentary

A GRAND NATIONAL COMMENTARY

By J. K. PYE

FOREWORD BY JOHN HISLOP

J. A. Allen & Co Ltd
1 Lower Grosvenor Place, London SW1

First published in 1971
by J. A. Allen & Co. Ltd.
1 Lower Grosvenor Place,
London, S.W.1.

© J. K. Pye

SBN 85131121 0

ACKNOWLEDGEMENTS
I am indebted to the Stewards of The Jockey Club for allowing me to quote from the Rules of Racing, to Mrs. M. Topham for permitting me to go over the Aintree Course on numerous occasions and, not least, to Mr. Ian Park of *The Liverpool Daily Post* for making many of the action photographs available for reproduction in the pages which follow.

J.K.P.

Printed by photo-lithography
and made in Great Britain at the
Pitman Press, Bath

Contents

Foreword

1.	The Course—Aintree then and now	1
2.	The Conditions of Entry and The Handicap	15
3.	Hat Pins and Hunches	21
4.	Theory and Practice	31
5.	Chance and Coincidence	57
6.	National Heroes	73
7.	The Changing Shape of The National	93
8.	The Winners and Placed Horses, 1837–1970	105
	Index	120

Foreword

No race has captured the public imagination more than the Grand National, and with the advent of television world-wide interest in it has become even greater. Thus there is a vast public eager for information on every aspect of the Grand National: its history, the changes that have taken place in it and the drama and anecdotes surrounding it. All this is found in Mr. Pye's classic work.

With its many excellent photographs and diagrams, the book gives a full picture of the greatest of all steeplechases and is a notable contribution to its bibliography.

John Hislop

Illustrations

The present lay-out of Aintree	8
The approach to the second fence	10
The first open ditch—fence No. 3 (19)	
Fence No. 4 (20). Becher's Brook	
Becher's Brook. Becher's Brook	
Becher's Brook. Fence No. 7 (23)	11
The Canal Turn fence	
Valentine's Brook. Fence No. 11 (27)	
"As they come onto the Racecourse"	
Moifaa. Ascetic's Silver. Lutteur III.	19
Shaun Spadah	
Music Hall. Gregalach	23
Shaun Goilin. Grackle	28
The Start in 1968	32
The Start in 1951	34
The false Start in 1952	
The first fence 1951	36
The first fence 1952	38
The first fence 1952	39
The first open ditch 1939	40
Becher's 1935	43
Becher's 1964	44
Becher's 1965	45
The first Canal Turn 1930	47
The first Canal Turn 1966	48
The Canal Turn 1953	
The Chair fence 1961	51
The Water jump 1951	
The Water jump 1955	
The Water jump 1956	53
At the end of the first circuit 1948	55
The first Valentine's 1926	59
The 27th 1927	
Grifel at Becher's	60
Becher's on the first circuit 1955	61
May King at Becher's 1930	62
Red Alligator at Becher's 1968	63
Trentino at Becher's 1923	64
The second Becher's 1970	65
Flying Wild at the Chair	67
Fujino-O at the Chair 1966	
The 23rd fence 1967	
The last fence 1951	
The last fence 1928	69
The *Devon Loch* drama	71
Cloister. Manifesto. Ambush II.	
Jerry M. Covercoat. Poethlyn	
Troytown. Sgt. Murphy. Sprig. Kellsboro'	81
Jack. Golden Miller. Reynoldstown.	
Battleship. Freebooter. Teal. Early Mist.	
Royal Tan. Quare Times	
E.S.B. Sundew. Oxo. Merryman II.	89
Jay Trump	
Battleship beats *Royal Danieli*	95
Red Alligator wins by 20 lengths	
Oxo wins from *Wyndburgh*	96
Team Spirit wins from *Purple Silk*	97
Ayala wins from *Carrickbeg*	99
Nicolaus Silver wins in 1961	
Royal Tan beats *Tudor Line*	103
The finish of the 1971 National	104

1.
The Course—
Aintree then and now

The course is obviously the major factor which shapes the race and its reputation as the most severe test of horse and rider. In fact the course and the race have become so synonymous that three years ago the Stewards of the National Hunt Committee, as it was then, stated that the National would never be run anywhere except at Aintree. But then the National would not be the National run anywhere except at Aintree.

    The extra inches in height of the fences above the minimum required, the difference in levels of take-off and landing sides, the variety and substance of the fences, the extreme distance of 4 miles 856 yards which contains them—all these are collectively embodied in one word—Aintree—and Aintree is the structure which has given shape to the various race patterns of the Grand National Steeplechases.

In Origin. According to a contributor to Blaine's 'Encyclopaedia of Rural Sports' Steeplechasing was born in the early part of the nineteenth century on a Leicestershire hunting field when, after a fruitless day, one of the riders suggested a race to the church spire at Melton which could just be seen in the distance. The result was not recorded but the promoter of the race observed what great sport it was 'without those . . . hounds'.

The writer goes on to state that whereas Don Quixote chose a windmill the Racing fraternity have chosen a steeple, but doubtless both pursuits are equally scurrilous!

The sport grew and acquired spectators and their demands to see both start and finish and all the incidents in between, were instrumental in the Steeplechase being brought on to the Racecourse.

1839. A description of one such Steeplechase course in 1839 was as follows:

The start . . . was on the side furthest from the Grandstand. The exit is sufficiently broad and is into a lane divided from the pasture-fields by a high bank, partly railed, partly topped with gorse and hawthorn. Through the first three or four pasture-fields there was nothing but extremely light fencing.

. . . The first obstacle that wore the aspect of a teaser was a deep ditch, above 5 ft wide, on the further side of which was a high bank. They were presently labouring through a deep, light soil, from which young wheat was springing. They next dashed over a high bank into a grass field which was a very wide one and one half of it had been recently subjected to deep ploughing. The fence opposite the field now was one of the most awkward of the series. First there was a strong paling, next a rough, high jagged hedge, and lastly a brook about 6 ft wide. . . . Some play was made across a smooth pasture-field, from whence, by a flying leap over a hedge, the riders were carried into a roughly ploughed field. Another hedge. . . . After clearing the hedge it was necessary immediately to turn short round to the left. At a distance of not more than 20 yards was a high hedge, bank and rails on the other side of which was a piece of water, let in for the purpose, full 15 ft wide, the field adjoining which is 6 ft lower than that from which the leap was to be taken.

The next leap was a particularly ugly one, into a field which was higher by 4 ft in some places than that from which the horses had to spring. They had to pass over a bank surmounted by a low hedge (in some places a strong rail), next to which was a ditch fenced by another rail. . . . From this point it was plain sailing across easy fences to the lower end of the racecourse. Here, turning to the left, the horses were brought by a straight run into the training ground, at the upper end of which was a stone wall 5 ft high, erected for the occasion. This was exactly opposite to the Grandstand. . . . After this straining task of more than two miles the horses had to gallop about half a mile to the starting point and then go over the severe ground a second time. . . . There was whip-and-spur work for the lead across the fields at the corner of the course leading to the run-in, across which a line of hurdles had been placed.

The course was Aintree and the race was the third Grand National Steeplechase, but which was known as The Grand Liverpool Steeplechase. Its present title was first used in 1847.

Changes. During the one hundred and thirty years which span the life of the National various changes have been made to the course over which it is run, but for the most part it has retained its basic characteristics and layout, and the changes have been chiefly to the composition of the fences rather than their placing.

The stone-wall fence referred to above was included to encourage entries from Ireland, and an ox-fence to tempt the Leicestershire entries. In 1840 the wall was lowered to 4 ft 6 in and the following year disappeared altogether, but re-appeared once or twice again after 1843.

Of the course in 1845, Finch Mason wrote:

Since the preceding year, sundry alterations had been made. There was then one field of turf on leaving the course, and one previous to entering it. In the first of these the turf had been pared off by the plough, in the second by the spade and the square lumps of turf and soil being loosely scattered about, made it as uneven and distressing a piece of ground for horses to gallop over as is possible to conceive.

Every other field in the line was fallow, with the exception of the two previous to Becher's Brook which were of wheat. Several of the rails on the banks were removed, and the line was on the whole a decidedly easy one.

Finch Mason's reference to various fields shows how the original Steeplechase courses comprised natural country with only semi-artificial fences—fences which were the normal perimeters of a field and altered only slightly from their natural shape. The steeplechase was for hunters and was run over 'fair hunting country'.

The Drop Fence. The 'drop fence', as it is known today, had its origin in the natural difference in levels of the land where the field on the landing side or drop side was lower than that on the take-off side. So too the converse case produced a higher level on the landing-side, and Aintree once boasted a fence known as the 'Table fence'.

The lay-out of the present Aintree course shows the different fields which still exist.

In the early years there was no inside rail or running rail and the fences which were higher in some parts than others were only marked by a flag which the riders had to go outside. One year a rider was walking the course before the race and these differences in height became more obvious to him the further he progressed. He hit on the idea of marking the easiest part of each fence with a piece of paper so that he would see at a glance where to set his horse. Had his plan resulted in victory this would doubtless have been hailed as the origin of the paper-chase, but alas! our would-be hero was observed in his scheme by a fellow competitor who re-sited each piece of paper at the most difficult part of each fence with the inevitable consequence for his rival.

The first major alteration to the fences took place in 1863/4 when they were reduced in size. An extract from an account of the 1864 Grand National course was as follows:

The line was full of ploughed fields and in the back stretch by the canal there seemed to be nothing else. . . . Becher's Brook had been cleared out and cut sharp and sloping. The nastiest jump was out of a ploughed field near the canal over a rail, ditch and hedge with a bad take-off. The jump at the distance post seemed like a wattle of gorse and scotch fir and the hedge at the water jump was of the same texture with canvas on the inside. The water jump was not an unmerciful one.

About this time the course included no less than seven hurdles as part of the total thirty fences. They were hurdles as we know them today only a little more substantial.

On the other hand the plough-land in 1881 was excessive—and the drills were growing mangolds. Four years later it disappeared altogether only to reappear spasmodically until 1890 since when the race has been run entirely on turf except for the two tan patches at Melling Road and Anchor Bridge.

The Distance. There have been changes also as regards the distance over which the National has been run although it has always been in excess of four miles, and from about the time the race was first run completely on turf the distance has been as it is today.

The actual fences in 1885 were as follows:

On the first circuit there were 15 fences of which the first 12 were jumped again on the second circuit, and then after the 27th the course finished over 3 gorse hurdles.

1 and 16	Small gorse hurdle.
2 and 17	Thorn fence 5 ft with a 3 ft rail on take-off side.
3 and 18	2 ft guard rail in front of ditch 6 ft 8 in wide and 3 ft deep followed by a Thorn fence 4 ft 6 in.
4 and 19	Rail and fence, both 2 ft 6 in high about 18 in apart.
5 and 20	Hurdle, 3 ft 6 in high, bushed with gorse.
6 and 21	Becher's Brook. Thick Thorn fence, 4 ft 6 in high, with 2 ft 6 in guard rail. On landing side a natural brook 9 ft 6 in wide and 6 ft deep.
7 and 22	Thorn fence, 5 ft 6 in high, with 2 ft 6 in guard rail in front of it.
8 and 23	The Canal Turn. The jump was placed at the spot where the course made a 90° turn so that the horses had to make a sharp turn left immediately on landing. Thorn fence, 5 ft high, with a 2 ft guard rail in front of a 6 ft ditch on take-off side.
9 and 24	Valentine's Brook. Thorn fence, 5 ft high, with a 2 ft guard rail in front, and a 5 ft brook on landing side.
10 and 25	Gorse hurdle, 3 ft 6 in high.
11 and 26	Thorn fence, 4 ft 6 in high, 2 ft rail guarding a ditch 6 ft wide and 3 ft deep on take-off side.

6 The Course—Aintree then and now

12 and 27 Thorn fence, 5 ft high, with a 2 ft guard rail, and a 5 ft ditch on landing side.

13 Gorse hurdle, 3 ft 6 in high.

14 Thorn fence, 4 ft 6 in high and 2 ft wide, with a 2 ft rail guarding a 6 ft ditch on take-off side.

15 The Water jump 12 ft 3 in long 2 ft deep preceded by 2 ft Thorn fence.

28, 29 and 30 Gorse hurdles 3 ft 6 in high.

1961. The alteration to the fences in 1961 was a major one. Hitherto they had been virtually perpendicular, but for the 1961 National they were sloped away on the take-off sides and have been the same in the years since so that they now give a horse those extra two feet or so in which to gain enough height in the air to clear them. Previously, if a horse got too close to them or 'underneath' them it stood no chance at all.

The effect which this leniency has had relates to an increased number of horses surviving into the second circuit.

Somewhat surprisingly the time for the race has hardly been affected at all.

Aintree now. A left-handed course, Aintree is set out on land which is best described as flat and although two gradients do come into the reckoning both are gradual. The first is from Becher's to the Canal and is downhill, and the second is from the last fence to the winning-post and is uphill.

The National course contains sixteen fences on the first circuit, of which the first fourteen are jumped again on the second circuit, and the two circuits measure 4 miles 856 yards.

The Start is still in front of the Stands and almost straight away the runners pass over a tan covered intersection made by the course and the Melling Road which on non-racing days is a public thoroughfare. Shortly after this the Flat course goes off to the left in its oval shape and the National course carries on in a straight line north-eastwards. From the point where the two courses separate the runners are said to 'go out into the country'.

As will be seen from the lay-out of the course the circuit starts with a line of six fences then the solitary fence No. 7 followed by a line of five fences down to the twelfth and finally the four fences practically in front of the Stands.

The Jockey Club's requirements concerning fences can be summarized as follows:

All fences must be at least 4 ft 6 in except the Water jump which must be at least 12 ft wide and 2 ft deep guarded by a fence not exceeding 3 ft in height and all plain fences must be the same in appearance on any one course. Plain fences must be made entirely of birch or birch brought out with gorse. (At Aintree, however, they are by custom built from hawthorn and dressed with spruce, fir or gorse and are known as Thorn fences.)

In addition there must be at least twelve fences in the first two miles of a steeplechase course and six for every succeeding mile. For every mile there must be a ditch 6 ft wide and 2 ft deep on the take-off side of a fence guarded by a bank and rail not exceeding 2 ft in height.

Becher's. As well known as The National itself Becher's got its name from the renowned Capt. Becher. The gallant Captain was leading the field in the race of 1839 when his horse fell at this fence which was described in the contemporary report as 'a strong paling, next a rough, high jagged hedge, and lastly a brook about 6 ft wide'. To avoid the oncoming horses which were strung out, Capt. Becher stayed where he had fallen—in the brook. He caught his horse and remounted only to fall again a few fences further at what is now Valentine's, and once more had a taste of water.

Becher's today is made up of a thorn fence of 4 ft 10 in and a brook of 5 ft 6 in. From the approach side the fence is not as forbidding as 'The Chair' fence nor any higher than the two previous fences, 4 and 5, but the view from mid-air of the drop-side is breathtaking to say the least. The way a horse copes with this difference in the levels of the two sides is a measure of his intelligence as well as his ability.

Both Becher's and the fence after it are at approximately 70° to the line of approach.

A Line of Country. Standing beyond Becher's and looking back down the line of six fences towards the Stands it is possible to get a very clear impression of the

8   The Course—Aintree then and now

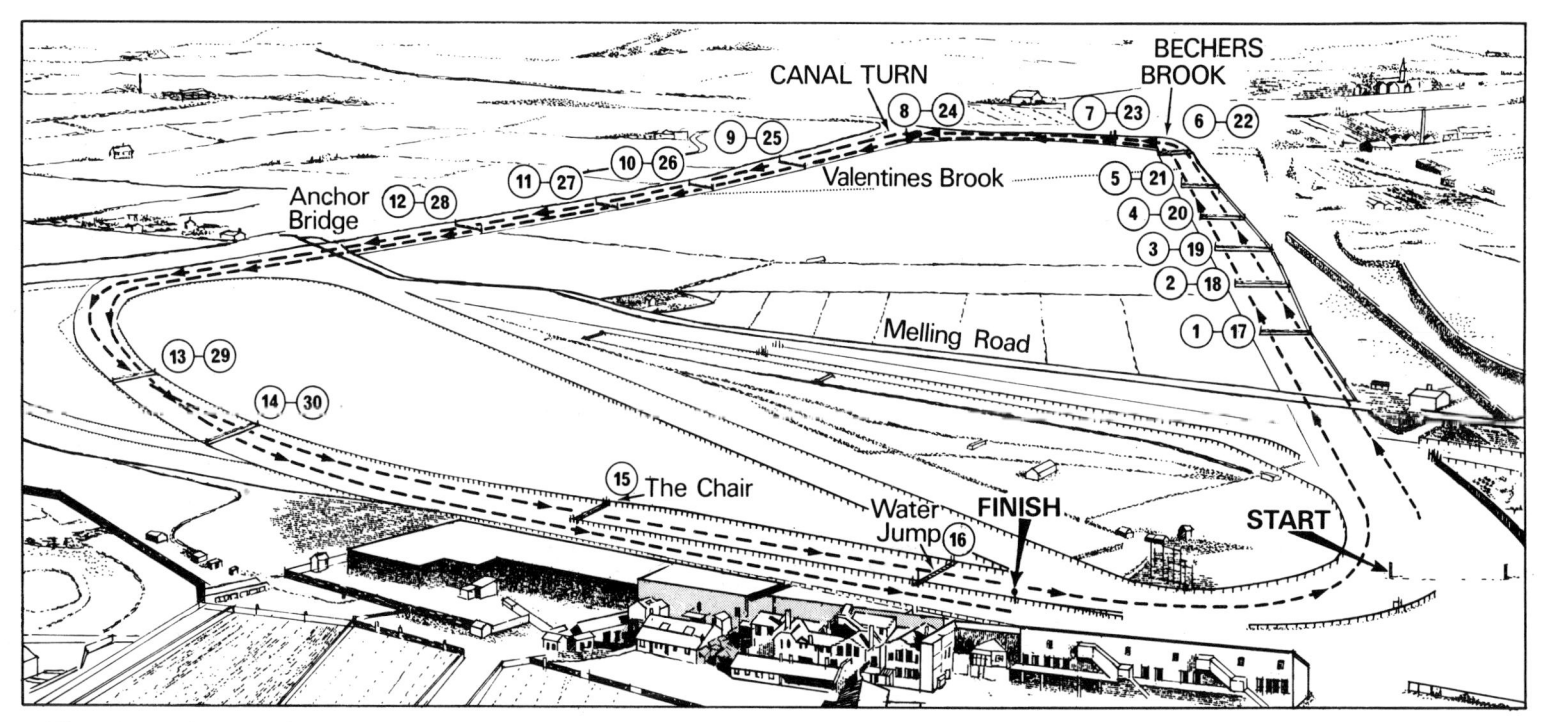

1 The present lay-out of Aintree.

THE KEY TO THE FENCES

1/17 Thorn fence 4 ft 6 in high dressed with gorse.

2/18 Thorn fence 4 ft 7 in high dressed with gorse.

3/19 Open ditch. Ditch 6 ft, fence 5 ft, dressed with spruce and banked up to an 18 in guard rail.

4/20 Thorn fence 4 ft 10 in high dressed with fir.

5/21 Thorn fence 4 ft 11 in high dressed with fir.

6/22 "Becher's Brook", 4 ft 10 in fence dressed with spruce followed by 5 ft 6 in brook.

7/23 Thorn fence 4 ft 6 in high dressed with fir.

8/24 "The Canal Turn Fence". Thorn fence 5 ft, dressed with fir.

9/25 "Valentine's Brook". 5 ft thorn fence dressed with spruce followed by a brook of 5 ft 6 in.

10/26 Thorn fence 5 ft high dressed with fir.

11/27 An open ditch. 6 ft ditch followed by 5 ft thorn fence dressed with fir.

12/28 5 ft thorn fence dressed with gorse followed by a ditch 5 ft 6 in wide.

13/29 Thorn fence 4 ft 7 in high dressed with gorse.

14/30 Thorn fence 4 ft 6 in high dressed with gorse.

15 "The Chair" fence. An open ditch; ditch 6 ft, followed by a thorn fence of 5 ft 2 in dressed with spruce.

16 The Water, 2 ft 6 in hedge fence followed by 12 ft 6 in spread of water 2 ft deep, 14 ft 9 in overall.

From the Starting Post to the first fence is 471 yards and from the last fence to the Winning Post is 494 yards.

immensity of the course for this section is but one fifth of the thirty fences which have to be jumped and the four and a half miles which have to be covered—by the winner at least.

The Canal Turn. The feature of the fence at the Canal Turn is the 90° turn immediately after the fence itself.

Many riders meet the fence at an angle in an attempt to save ground and so that they land with the turn on the far side of the fence half completed, but in asking the horse to jump the obstacle in this way they are asking him to do something unfamiliar and, in addition, they are making the jump longer. Either, or both of these have been the cause of many of the casualties at this fence which was an open ditch until 1929, since when it has been a Thorn fence.

At one period the only barrier between the Canal and the course was the usual outside running rail and in the past loose horses have jumped fence No. 8 and gone straight on to jump the running rail and landed in the Canal, but this is no longer possible.

Valentine's. The brook fence (fence No. 9) on the other side of the course to Becher's got its name in 1840. Mr. Power, an Irish amateur, was riding a horse called *Valentine* and he had struck a bet that he would be the first over the Wall fence in front of the Stands. At Becher's he was almost a furlong ahead of everything else except *Lottery*. Without slackening their pace they cleared the Canal Turn fence and approached the ninth. *Valentine* stopped, reared up on his hind legs and then half lunged, half corkscrewed over the fence. From that moment on it was Valentine's Brook. Horse and rider were first over the Wall fence and finally finished third.

8 to 12. The reputation which these fences have for being substantial is not ill-founded but it must be remembered that when a horse hits a fence it does so with a force which is made up of something like 12 cwts travelling at 25–30 m.p.h. Of the different sections of the course this group of fences (8, 9, 10, 11 and 12) is probably the stiffest as each of the five fences is 5 ft in height, and four out of the five have additional hazards. Fence No. 12 is at an angle of about 75° to the line of approach.

The Course—Aintree then and now

2 The approach to the second—a Thorn fence of 4 ft 7 in.

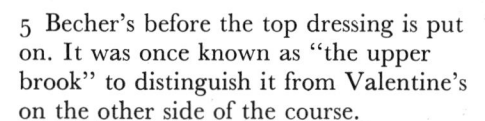

3 The take-off side of the first open-ditch fence No. 3(19).

4 Fence No. 4(20). It is slightly banked on the take-off side and has a drop on the landing side. The apron has been added to all the fences except the open ditches since 1961. Prior to which they were almost as upright as the fence in the previous illustration.

5 Becher's before the top dressing is put on. It was once known as "the upper brook" to distinguish it from Valentine's on the other side of the course.

6 Becher's taken from the opposite side of the fence with Valentine's in the background.

7 The core of Becher's before the top dressing is put on.

The Course—Aintree then and now 11

8 All ready for the big day—the approach to Becher's. The scaffolding in the background supports a T.V. camera and crew.

9 The approach to the Thorn fence after Becher's—fence No. 7(23) with the Canal Turn fence in the background.

10 The Canal Turn before its top dressing. Once known as The Pond Fence because of its proximity to the Canal. The wing of the fence is packed with fir so that the runners approaching the fence are not distracted by those already over it and going in a different direction.

12 After Valentine's there is a Thorn fence and then this open ditch—fence No. 11(27).

11 **Valentine's Brook**—fence No. 9(25). It used to be called "the lower brook".

13 "As they come onto the Racecourse . . .". On the first circuit they have eighteen fences to jump but on the second circuit only two.

The Anchor Bridge Crossing. The other intersection made by the Melling Road is also a tan covering over the road surface and is known as the Anchor Bridge Crossing. Immediately after the Crossing, which is between fences 12 and 13, the Flat and National courses meet up again and the runners are said 'to come back on to the Racecourse'.

The Chair Fence. Fence No. 15 is the biggest on the course and is known as 'The Chair Fence'. It is the third open ditch—the ditch of 6 ft being followed by a fence of 5 ft 2 in.

In the early days of Steeplechasing there was an official known as the 'Distance Judge'. He occupied a chair at the end of the fifteenth fence nearest the run-in and his function was to retire those horses which had not reached him by the time the winner passed the Winning Post. They were said to be 'distanced'. The current expression 'won by a distance' and 'at the distance marker', had their origins in these circumstances and the pedestal or dais which held the Distance Judge's chair is still on its original site by the fifteenth fence—hence its name 'The Chair fence'.

The Water. The first circuit ends with the Water jump, fence No. 16. This fence was described by Lord Sefton in 1852 as a 'very large but perfectly fair jump' and in the account of the 1864 National, referred to earlier, it was said to be 'not an unmerciful one' but many people contend that it is just that because the small fence of 2 ft 6 in which preceeds it is not high enough to promote a jump which is long enough to clear the Water. The probability is that a horse jumping short will injure its back.

After this last fence on the first circuit the runners swing round to the left past the Winning Post and then past the Starting Post and on towards the 17th which of course, was fence No. 1. The second circuit is the same as the first up to fence No. 30 after which they miss The Chair and The Water and cover the 494 yards of the run-in to the Winning Post. This part is slightly uphill and is dog-legged as it goes round fences 15 and 16.

The siting of the various fences at Aintree is no haphazard affair and only by considering the order in which they are placed and realising the bearing one fence has on another can the real character of the course be seen.

The drops on the landing side of the first two fences, whilst probably no great problem for a horse with previous experience of the course, are obstacles far beyond the novelty kind for the newcomer.

The third fence, the first open ditch, is banked on the approach side and is very similar to open ditches on other courses. If a horse has not yet got used to the idea of a lower landing side to the fences then the third, fourth and fifth will give him plenty of opportunity.

The misleading face of Becher's has already been mentioned but its guile has a consequence in fence No. 7. Apart from being on an elbow in the course this fence seems diminutive in the light of the recent experience of Becher's and for that very reason many horses have taken it too carelessly whilst those expecting a drop find none.

The Canal Turn has been mentioned already but the sequence of fences which follow deserves special mention.

Valentine's, fence No. 9, is the brook fence on the Canal side of the course. It is not as stiff as its counterpart Becher's, but it sets the scene for the fences which follow. Fence No. 10 is a plain Thorn fence 5 ft in height, whilst the next is the second open ditch. This, fence No. 11, is the same in dimensions as fence No. 3 except that there is a very big drop on the landing side and many jockeys consider this fence, coming as it does after three by no means easy jumps each 5 ft high, to be the most dangerous jump on the course. Another 5 ft Thorn fence followed by a ditch but a higher landing side constitutes fence No. 12, and then there is a long run of approximately half a mile to the next.

Conditioned to expecting lower landing sides by each of the fences from 8 to 11 the very absence of such a drop is the cause of many fallers at fences 13 and 14. The third open ditch, fence No. 15, although two inches higher than the two previous open ditches is outwardly much the same. It will be remembered that both had substantial drops, whereas, fence No. 15, The Chair fence, has a higher landing side.

Of the third open ditch, fence No. 15, John Hislop has written:

Even including Becher's and the last open ditch before the racecourse, the obstacle that makes my heart beat fastest as one nears it is the 'Chair'. It stands up against the skyline, grim, tall and formidable, the rail before it reminding one of the veritable moat that it guards, and the fence itself seeming as impenetrable as a prison wall.

In fact the fence is only two inches higher than the two previous open ditches but sited on the same rising ground parallel to the run-in it is higher on the landing side than take-off side and any fence situated on an uphill gradient is always that much more difficult than one on level ground. So, besides their substance and individual characteristics the order in which the fences are placed is an additional factor to be reckoned with.

2. The Conditions of Entry and The Handicap

'A handicap is a race in which the weights to be carried by the horses are adjusted by the Handicapper for the purposes of equalising their chances of winning'.

THE JOCKEY CLUB RULES

The Conditions of Entry. The advertised conditions of entry for the 1969 Grand National were as follows:

GRAND NATIONAL STEEPLECHASE (handicap) with £17,500 added to stakes: for horses which at closing and since November 1, 1966 have been placed first, second, third or fourth in a steeplechase of any distance over the Grand National Course at Aintree, or which within the same period have won a steeplechase of three miles or upwards of the advertised value of £500, or with at least £400 added to a sweepstakes (or the equivalent in foreign distance and money), or which have won a steeplechase of any distance value £600 to the winner (or the equivalent in foreign money), selling races in every case excepted; £10 to enter; £50 extra unless forfeit be declared by January 28, £20 extra unless forfeit be declared by March 11. £20 extra if declared to run; second 20 per cent, third 10 per cent, fourth 5 per cent of stakes. The Grand National Course, about four miles and 856 yards. The Horserace Betting Levy Board have given £10,000 and Messrs. Tophams Ltd. £7,500 (including a Gold Trophy value £1,500) included in the value of this race.

In addition the trainer of the winner will receive a Cup value £200 and the rider of the winner a Cup value £100, also £2,537 given by Messrs. Tophams Ltd. will be divided as follows:

£1,000 to the Trainer of the winner	£100 to the Trainer of the third.
*£500 to the Rider of the winner.	*£50 to the Rider of the third.
£250 to the Stable of the winner.	£25 to the Stable of the third.
£300 to the Trainer of the second.	£50 to the Trainer of the fourth.
*£150 to the Rider of the second.	*£25 to the Rider of the fourth.
£75 to the Stable of the second.	£12 to the Stable of the fourth.

The Grand National, being a handicap and the most valuable race in the National Hunt Calendar, has never lacked for runners, indeed there have been times when the race has suffered from oversized fields.

Any noticeable increase in the field for the National is usually the direct result of either, or both, of two events; firstly, the victory the previous year of a horse with

---

* These prizes do not apply to Amateur Riders. Trophies value £50 (£25 in the case of the fourth) will be awarded in lieu.

moderate form and, secondly, any marked increase in the value of the race.

In 1928 a horse whose chances were rated at 100/1 won the National. In fact only two finished from an original field of 42 and even the second horse had to be remounted. The Aintree Executive decided to forestall the expected spate of entries by increasing the amount of the entrance stake in the hope that owners of moderate horses would think twice about entering them.

However, owners and trainers construed this action as being merely intended to increase the value of the race. The prize was more coveted than ever and everyone with a staying 'chaser in training, and a good many who had anything but, entered their horses with the result that in 1929 sixty-six faced the Starter, whose comments, unfortunately, were not recorded.

Oversized fields invariably mean a large number of fallers which is the result of physical overcrowding and also the lower standard of ability of many horses which make up large fields.

Having failed to limit the size of field by increasing the cost of running a horse in the National to £100 the next move in this direction came in 1932 when the conditions of entry restricted the race to horses which had won or been placed in a race of three miles or over and worth at least £200 to the winner or a 'Chase over any distance at Liverpool.

That such a qualifying clause was overdue was self-evident for genuine sportsmen have always taken a greater pleasure in seeing horses jump well rather than fall, and this spectacle could only be achieved by ensuring that the race was contested by completely suitable runners.

The two points on which suitability must be judged are a horse's ability to cope with the peculiarities of thirty Aintree fences and its ability to get the four and a half miles of the National.

In what was regarded as the Golden Age in Steeplechasing in the 1870s and 1880s one of the most successful trainers was the Irishman, Henry Linde. At Eyrefield Lodge where he trained he had the major Aintree fences reproduced on his schooling grounds and when he sent a horse to Aintree he expected it not to fall regardless of where it finished in the placings. Two Grand National winners and several placed horses, as well as numerous winners of the lesser Aintree races, show that his expectancy was not mere optimism.

Many authorities decry this method of schooling on the grounds that too much constant strain is put upon the horse's tendons—in fact many of Linde's horses could not be kept sound.

On this topic of suitability of candidate it must be observed that the race only becomes 'a cruel race' when unsuitable horses are entered for it.

The Handicap. The weight range of the handicap is laid down in the Rules of Racing and at present the top weight is 12st. and the bottom weight 10st., but in the past it has been widely different to this. In 1857 for example it was 11st. 2lb.—8st. 10lb. and was much criticized because it meant that many leading riders could not do the weights. In consequence many who rode in the Nationals during this period were grooms with no experience of race riding.

At present a rider must have ridden at least five winners under the Rules of Racing or one of the corresponding codes which exist elsewhere before he can ride in the National.

As already mentioned, there has never been a shortage of runners for the National and the range of the handicap is one of the ways of curtailing the number of entries. At a time when the top weight was 12st. 7lb. and the bottom weight was about to be reduced from 10st. 7lb. to 10st., thereby introducing a range of 35lb., there was an outcry from owners and trainers and The Hon. Geo. Lambton wrote to the Press as follows:

Before the race this year I often heard it said that this was the most interesting National for many years. Why was it so interesting? Because good horses like *Golden Miller*, *Reynoldstown* and *Avenger* had their fair chance and were not crushed by weight. Even then we have seen that *Reynoldstown* would not have been able to give 23lb. to a tubed horse which has been beaten in selling races, so why go back to the 10st. limit? Two stone is enough to give away over that course, and if any owner thinks that he has no chance of beating one like *Reynoldstown* at 2st., then he should not aspire to win the Grand National. I have much sympathy for owners of bad horses (I have many of them myself), but we should not expect to win great races with

Left
14 Moiffa (1904).
15 Ascetic's Silver (1906)

Right
16 Lutteur III (1909).
17 Shaun Spadah (1921).

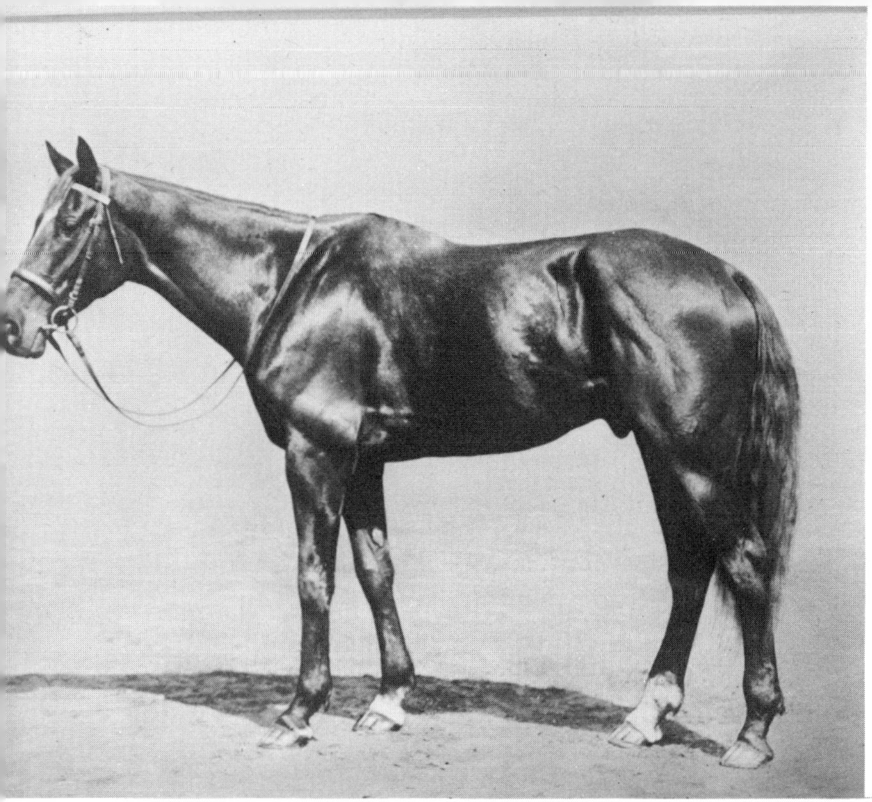

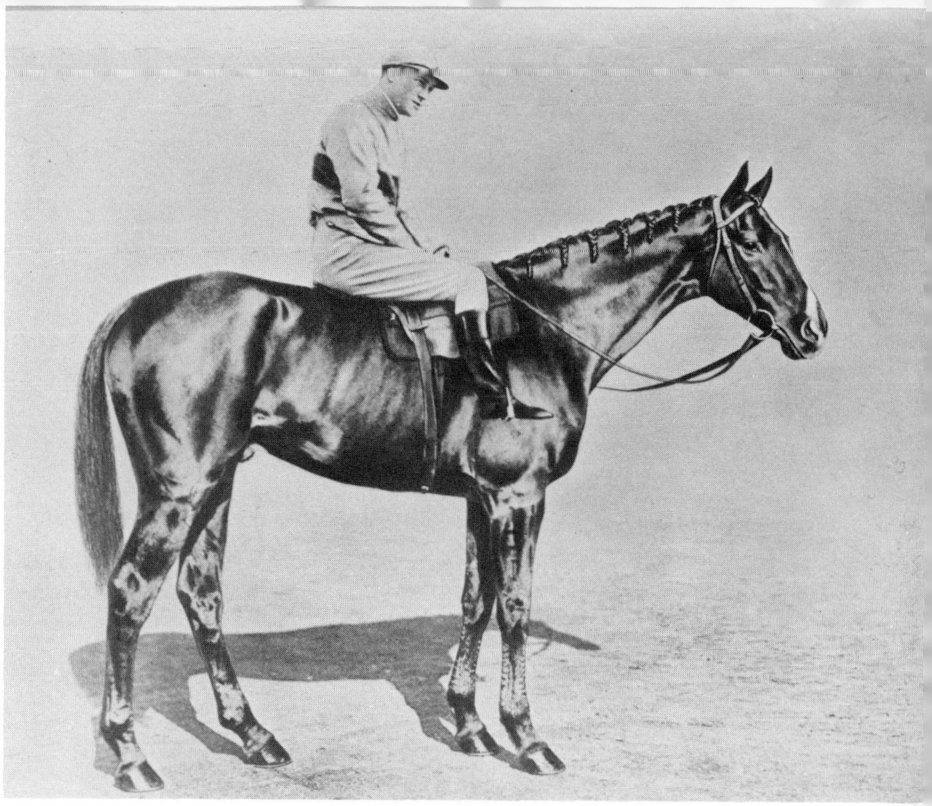

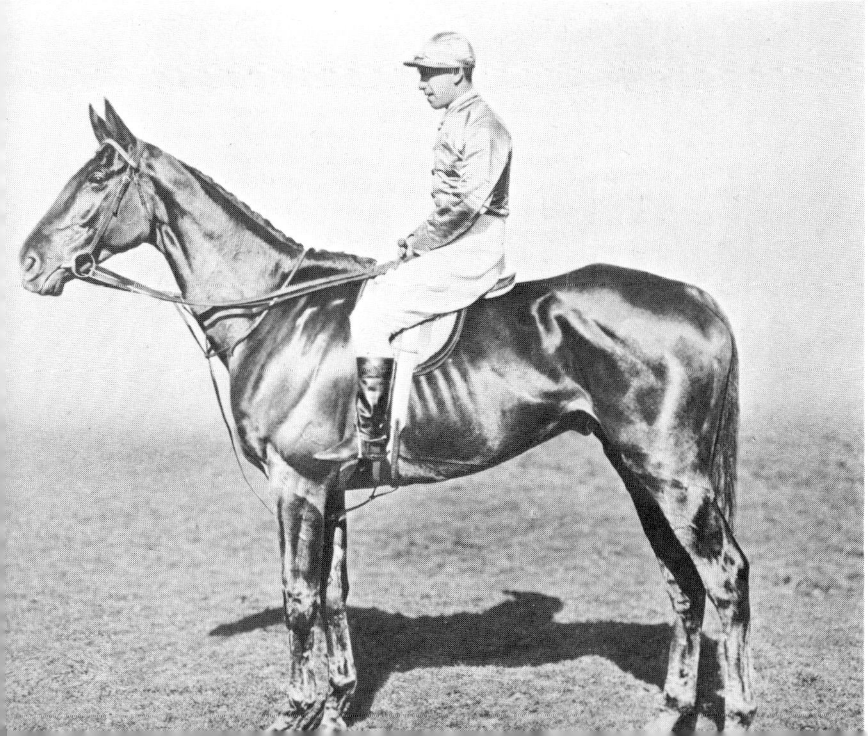

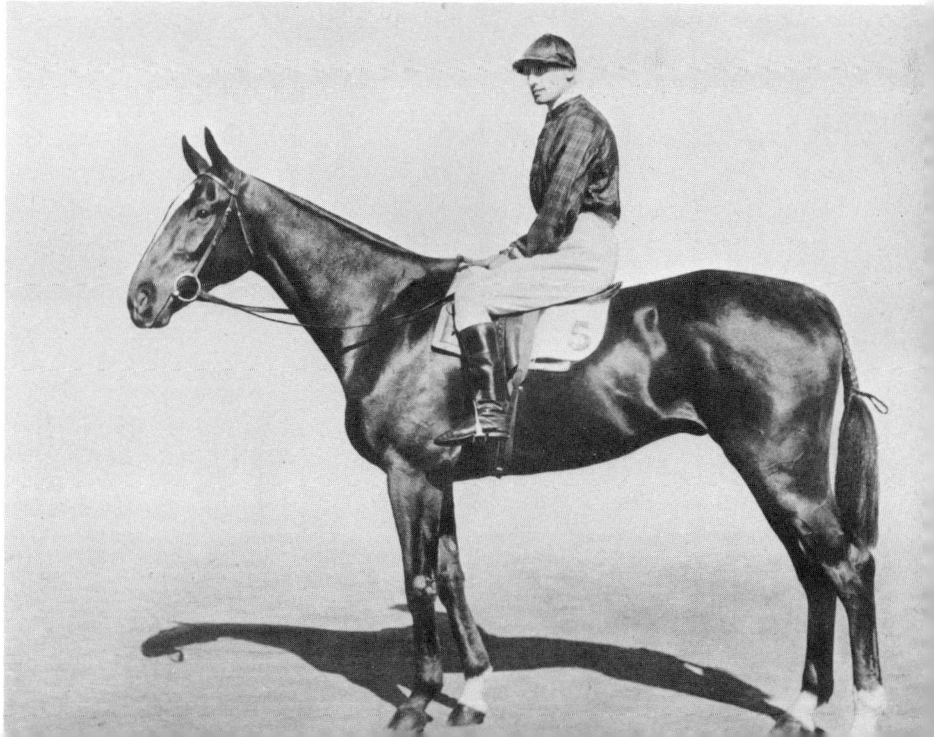
5

them. The Grand National is no place for bad horses. If the authorities encourage owners to enter them the race will lose its high tone and quality and revert to the farcical scramble it became some years ago.

For several successive years in the late 1950s the range of the handicap was made to look as though it was 14lb. instead of 28lb. by the withdrawal of the top weighted horses.

To counteract this Rule 95(d) was brought into force and it reads as follows:

If, in the opinion of the handicapper, not more than two of the horses entered are a clear 14lb. better than the rest of the entry, the handicapper shall frame his handicap down to 21lb. below the permitted lowest weight. In these handicaps when the highest original handicap weight of horses declared to run under Rule 120(i) is less than 12st. in the Liverpool Grand National Steeplechase it shall be raised to that weight and the other weights increased accordingly.

Those horses handicapped below 10st. do in fact carry that weight in the race.

A weight range of 28lb. can be shown in a handicap with a top weight of 12st. 7lb. and a bottom weight of 10st. 7lb. as it can in a handicap of 12st.–10st. but time and again a weight in excess of 12st. has proved the undoing of good horses like *Prince Regent* and others and has been one of the reasons why many good horses have not been risked at Aintree.

The reshaping of the fences in 1961 was a step towards attracting good horses and was simultaneous with a new handicap weight range of 12st.–10st. which has been the same ever since except for a short period and is a much fairer proposition. Even so, and with a prize far greater than any other under National Hunt Rules, Aintree still failed to attract such horses as *Arkle* and *Mill House*.

3. Hat Pins and Hunches

'Ye lads who love a steeplechase and danger
freely court, sirs,
Hark forward all to Liverpool to join the
gallant sport, sirs,
The English and the Irish nags are ready for
the fray, sirs,
And which may lose and which may win, 'tis
very hard to say, sirs.

Old song

Watching the horses being led round the Paddock before the National each is easily identified by its name-cloth, but identifying it is one thing and recognising it as the winner at this stage is another.

Amongst themselves Grand National winners have been as varied as it is possible to imagine, some as tall as 17 hands and others barely 15·2. They have been as young as 5 and as old as 13. The majority of them have been geldings but mares and entires have won it as well. Browns, blacks, chesnuts, bays and greys have all won as well as *Lottery* who was described as 'mealy brown'. Full sisters and half-brothers have won it and so have one hundred and twenty odd others with no immediate parentage in common at all.

Such a variety of type is proof that the National winners do not form a genus or species with any distinguishing feature except that of courage.

Height. *Troytown* and *Moifaa* were both 17 hands or more but *Abd-el-Kader* and *The Lamb* were a mere 15·2, whilst the bulk of the National winners have been 16–16·2. Thus, size is no handicap nor is lack of it a bar to winning the race—within reason.

The Conformation of 'the typical Aintree horse'. In spite of the victories of such small horses as *The Lamb*, *Abd-el-Kader* and *Battleship* there is a popular fallacy that a horse has to be exceptionally tall to jump the Aintree fences. The bigger the horse the greater seems to be the certainty that it is 'a typical Aintree candidate'. On the evidence of conformation alone it is impossible to predict of any horse that it will cope with the National fences or distance. Conformation can only show plenty of heart room and depth and a good sloping shoulder. One can go on . . . a good bold head, closely coupled etc., etc., but one still ends up with 'handsome is as handsome does', and in the past it has not been unknown for a camel to have been preferred purely on looks to a horse which won the National, but to save the winner of 1904 embarrassment, he will not be mentioned by name.

Nor was he alone in this respect for the first time Nightingall was engaged to ride *Ilex* at Nottingham in 1888 one of the jockey's friends was so appalled at the make

18 Music Hall (1922).

19 Gregalach (1929).

and shape of the horse when he saw it in the parade ring that he begged Nightingall not to ride it and backed his pleas with the offer of a £5 note so concerned was he for the rider's safety. *Ilex* won the race handsomely and two years later the partnership was successful in the National. In 1891 and 1892 *Ilex*, again ridden by Nightingall, finished third and in both these years *Cloister* was second.

Looking at the equine members of the parade ring at Aintree it is easy to see what inspired Will Ogilvie to write:

> And the limber lean-of-head ones,
> Hardy, hefty, humble-bred ones

When the photographs of National winners appear in the various periodicals and journals after the race one can with a minimum of imagination relate the conformation of the horse to his achievement in winning, but anyone who claims to be able to do this before the race lays himself open to charges of vanity or insanity, or both.

Action. A horse's action can be most indicative of his winning chances especially if there is any evidence of his or her ability to produce an extra leg in emergency for as sure as a horse sets foot on Aintree it will meet at least one such emergency, and the ability to produce this additional limb when needed is essential to cope with a crisis of balance.

So, from looks and action one can expect little help.

Colour. Three Grand Nationals have been won by grey horses—two by *The Lamb* (1868/71) and one by *Nicolaus Silver* (1961). This probably is a fair reflection of the number of grey horses (in proportion to the other colours) which have run in the National. *The Colonel* (1869/70) and *Royal Mail* (1937) were both black horses, as was *Reynoldstown*. The majority of National winners have been bay, brown or chesnut.

Only two blinkered horses have ever won the race—*Foinavon* and *Battleship*.

Age. *Regal* (1876) was a five-year-old and *Why Not* (1894) was a thirteen-year-old when they won.

The ages of the National winners have been as follows:

26 have been termed 'aged', i.e. anything over 6.

5 ,,	,, aged 5	13 ,,	,, aged 8	6 ,,	,, aged 11
16 ,,	,, aged 6	31 ,,	,, aged 9	3 ,,	,, aged 12
17 ,,	,, aged 7	9 ,,	,, aged 10	2 ,,	,, aged 13

Whereas it was often the practice to send a horse to Liverpool as young as five or six, nowadays even seven is considered too young and few trainers will risk a horse at Aintree before he reaches eight or nine. A converse view is expressed in the words 'If he's good enough he's old enough'.

However, the last seven-year-old to win was *Bogskar* in 1940 since when all the winners have been eight or over. *Lutteur III* was the last five-year-old to win in 1909 previous to which one has to go as far back as 1880 the year the brilliant Irish mare *Empress* won. The last successful six-year-old was *Ambush II* in 1900.

The Breeding of National Winners. There have only been two cases of half-brothers and one case of full sisters winning the National. *Vanguard* (1843) and *Pioneer* (1846) were half brothers; *Emblem* and *Emblematic* (1863 and 1864) were full sisters who won in successive years. By strange coincidence *Arbury* was second to both of them. *Anglo* (1966) and *Red Alligator* (1968) were also half-brothers. So the chances of a half-brother or half-sister to a previous winner winning the race are not outstanding.

Ascetic, *My Prince* and *Cottage* all sired three National winners and *Jackdaw* sired two, and the winner is frequently sired by a horse which is in the top six in the leading Sires of jumpers. Up to the time of writing *Vulgan* also has sired three National winners.

Sex. The National has been won several times by entire horses amongst them *Wanderer* (1855), *Free Trader* (1856), *Half Caste* (1859), *Disturbance* (1873), *Reugny* (1874), *Austerlitz* (1877) *Shifnal* (1878), and the most recent one was *Battleship* in 1938.

Mares which won the National were *Miss Mowbray* (1856), *Anatis* (1860), *Jealousy* (1861), *Emblem* (1863), *Emblematic* (1864), *Casse Tete* (1872), *Empress* (1880), *Zoedone* (1883), *Frigate* (1889), *Shannon Lass* (1902), *Sheila's Cottage* (1948) and *Nickel Coin* (1951). Thus the bulk of the National winners have been geldings.

Weight. Since the race became a handicap in 1843 only *Cloister* (12st. 7lb.), *Manifesto* (12st. 7lb.), *Jerry M* (12st. 7lb.), *Poethlyn* (12st. 7lb.), *Sprig* (12st. 4lb.), *Golden Miller* (12st. 2lb.) and *Reynoldstown* (12st. 2lb.), have carried more than 12st. and won. The lowest weighted horse to win was *Free Trader* carrying 9st. 6lb. in 1856.

Since 1946 12 winners have carried a weight between 10st.–10st. 7lb.; 6 have come from the 10st. 8lb.–11st. bracket; 6 from the range of 11st. 1lb. to 11st. 7lb., and only *Freebooter* (11st. 11lb.) won with more than 11st. 8lb.

Form and the National. Form is of little value unless it is Aintree form. The distance of the race and the nature of the fences make form on any other course indicative only of one horse's chances against another's on similar courses. Aintree is so different that only Aintree can produce the evidence which is applicable to the National. In the past many National winners had been placed previously in the race before they won or had shown strong evidence of ability over the course. *Cloister, Manifesto, Jerry M* are the arch examples and in recent years *Freebooter* was another example. Even a glimpse of a horse's ability to jump the course and stay the distance *and* his liking for the job is worth more than an unbeaten record in fifty races elsewhere.

In view of the fact that Aintree is such a specialist's course it is somewhat surprising at first sight that only six have won the race twice.

The dual winners. *Peter Simple* (1849/53), *Abd-el-Kader* (1850/1), *The Lamb* (1868/71), *The Colonel* (1869/70), *Manifesto* (1897/99), *Reynoldstown* (1935/6).

Abd-el-Kader was the first to win two Nationals and *Manifesto* came the closest to winning three. In 130 years no horse ever has won three but as long as there are three Nationals to be won it isn't impossible.

However, these six must be credited with twelve races and to them must be added many more which came close to winning twice either previously, or subsequently, to winning once. *Miss Mowbray* was second the year after she won; *Free Trader* was second the year before he won and a host of others down to *Cloister* who was second twice before he won. *Frigate* was second three times before winning.

But even this pointer is limited in its application for many horses such as *Seventy-Four*, *The Knight of Gwynne*, and in more recent years *Irish Lizard*, *Wynburgh* and *Freddie*, were all placed more than once but never succeeded in winning. Others have gone on trying and finally have succeeded, such as *Team Spirit* who had failed to show any worthwhile form at Aintree in three Nationals and then finished fourth before he finally won at his fifth attempt at the age of twelve.

Conversely, *Voluptuary* and *Alcibiade* had not run in a Steeplechase of any kind before they won the National, but it must be remembered that Aintree in the 1860s and onwards was not the stiff Aintree of today and the course at that time had seven hurdles in its thirty obstacles. Even in recent years horses have won the National at their very first attempt at Aintree—*Jay Trump* was one, but they are the exceptions rather than the rule.

Backing the Jockey. In 1905 the first horse past the post in the Grand National was *Ascetic's Silver* but the records show that he won the race in 1906, In 1905 although he did beat *Kirkland* he had unfortunately parted company with his rider at the third fence, and whilst *Ascetic's Silver* found his own way round it is stipulated that a horse must have a rider! In some cases they are a hindrance to the horse whilst in others they are an asset, and one can have worse reasons for backing a horse in the National than because its rider has had experience of the course or, better still, success in the race.

Riders who have distinguished themselves over the big ones at Aintree are headed by George Stevens with five victories. Tom Olliver is credited with four successes from eighteen National rides. A. Nightingall rode the winner in three Nationals.

Mr. Tommy Pickernell, who rode under the name of 'Mr. Thomas' in no less than 17 Nationals had three winning mounts one of which was *Pathfinder*. This horse was

20 Shaun Goilin 1930

21 Grakle 1931

rather aptly named. At the end of a glorious career in the saddle 'Mr. Thomas' was in the habit of indulging in the contents of his flask before racing. On this occasion he must have forgotten to say 'when' for as the jockeys were told to line up he faced the wrong way. However, *Pathfinder* lived up to its name and turned round in time.

Mr. Tommy Beasley also rode three winners, as did Mr. Jack Anthony before he turned professional, and the following were associated with two winners each— C. Green, Mr. A. Goodman, J. Page, Mr. J. Richardson, Mr. E. Wilson, Percy Woodland, Arthur Thompson, E. Piggott, Bryan Marshall, Fred Winter and Pat Taaffe who has had seventeen rides in the race. George Stevens (twice), Mr. T. Beasley, Mr. Richardson, Mr. E. Wilson and Bryan Marshall are the only riders to have ridden the winner in successive years. Mr. Alex Goodman was 30 when he rode his first National winner and 44 when he won on *Salamander*. Bruce Hobbs was 17 when he rode *Battleship* to win and Jack Anthony was the same age when he won on the one-eyed *Glenside*.

Trainers, also, have proved worth following in the past and in the Post-War years Vincent O'Brien has saddled the winner in three consecutive years (a distinction which has never been achieved before although Linde nearly did for having won with *Empress* and *Woodbrook*, his *Cyrus* ran second to *Seaman* in 1882). Capt. Neville Crump and T. F. Rimell have each trained three National winners 'though not in successive years.

Many people back a horse in the National merely because they like its name and always plunge for one with 'town' in it—*Jenkinstown*, *Troytown*, *Reynoldstown*—or one which has the word 'cottage' as part of it—*Sheila's Cottage*, *Lovely Cottage* and if there is ever a horse called *Cottagetown* it is certain to start favourite. Unusual names have had their supporters—*Mr. What* for example or *Quare Times* and present day race-commentators can thank their lucky stars they did not have to cope with *Cushalu Mavourneen* or *Hornihiharriho* or were faced with two horses called *Pioneer* which there were in the National of 1848. To confuse everyone in 1902 and 1903 there were two horses called *Drumcree* and *Drumree*.

As a last resort there is the time-honoured hat-pin.

But before backing your selection with something stronger than words remember to do so in moderation for as Jack Leach has said—an occupational hazard in backing Steeplechasers is the fact that your money, when it isn't in the air, is on the floor.

Finally, whether you use a hat-pin or play a hunch rest assured that the winner is in the Paddock somewhere for every intended runner must do at least one circuit of this green rectangle before going to Post.

Just for the Record. *Golden Miller's* time of 9 mins. $20\frac{2}{5}$ secs. carrying 12st. 2lb. represents an average speed for the 4 miles 856 yards of 28.8 m.p.h.

The 66 strong field in 1929 was a record size for Racing in England either on the Flat or National Hunt.

The smallest field for the National was the year of its inception when 6 started.

Value. In 1837 the race was a Sweepstakes of 25 sovs. each with 100 sovs. added. Since 1929 the Sweepstake has been 100 sovs. and the added money has been increased at various times to the present £17,500. The richest ever National was won by Anglo in 1966 and was worth £22,334 to his owner.

4. Theory and Practice

'You'd better let me let the horse go along gentlemen, and not upset him; he'll take a deal more out of himself by waiting'.

DICK CHRISTIAN'S LECTURE IN
'THE POST AND THE PADDOCK'

22 The level Start of 1968.

The Parade. It has been said that the tension in the weighing-room before the National is so great that it is possible to hear a pin drop, but one would have thought that the noise made by all those butterflies would make it difficult to hear anything drop—even those breathtaking words for which everyone has been waiting—'Jockeys out!'

Many trainers do not believe in giving last minute instructions on the grounds that good jockeys don't need them and bad ones don't heed them. Perhaps the most one can say in the circumstances is to repeat Maunsell Richardson's advice which was to 'go for the blackest part of every fence'.

Another theory, which is attributed to Count Kinsky's groom as the amateur rider was put into the saddle on *Zoedone*, was 'Hunt on the first circuit and then, and not before, start to race'.

Bryan Marshall always liked to go the shortest possible way round, and Arthur Thompson preferred to be out in front.

What goes through a jockey's mind as he and his horse are led out from the Paddock to parade in front of the Stands? This is the richest, the longest and the toughest race in the National Hunt Calendar, and it is every rider's ambition to win it.

The thought which is uppermost in most jockey's minds is wondering what the next fifteen minutes will have in store for them. Their chances of completing the course are not bright—3 or 4 to 1 against. As they parade in lines past the bookmakers' boards they may catch the odds being called and many a jockey must have been sorely tempted to take them, but a jockey is not supposed to bet.

One year, so the story goes, Dave Dick spotted a banner amongst the crowd which read 'Repent, or your sins will find you out'. 'In that case', said the jockey, 'I won't reach the first fence'.

Or perhaps a rider will remember the words of Gerry Wilson who rode *Golden Miller* in 1934:

I was only frightened once in my career and that was in the National in the nineteen-thirties. Jack Molony was riding Lord Bicester's *K.G.B.* and at the open ditch after Valentine's the first time round he refused and baulked my mount *Delarue*, both horses falling into the ditch with Jack and I between them. There were some thirty-odd horses behind us, and you can imagine what it felt like, crouching down in the ditch, and seeing horses and bellies going over our heads. The noise was terrific as they hit the guard rail.

Omens, Dreams, etc. Superstition also plays a part in the pre-race make-up of those involved in the National—sometimes to a ridiculous extent. Not all that long ago a trainer with one National winner to his credit had his horse removed to another box in the stable yard at Aintree because the first box had been already occupied by a National winner some years previously, and presumably he was a firm believer in lightning's alleged characteristic of being averse to striking the same spot twice. However, the horse won but history has not recorded whether the trainer attributed its success to his own training abilities or his superstitious nature. In any event he was credited with the stake in the list of Winning Trainers, and he would doubtless be surprised to learn, were he still alive, that Box No. 4 in the New Yard at Liverpool,

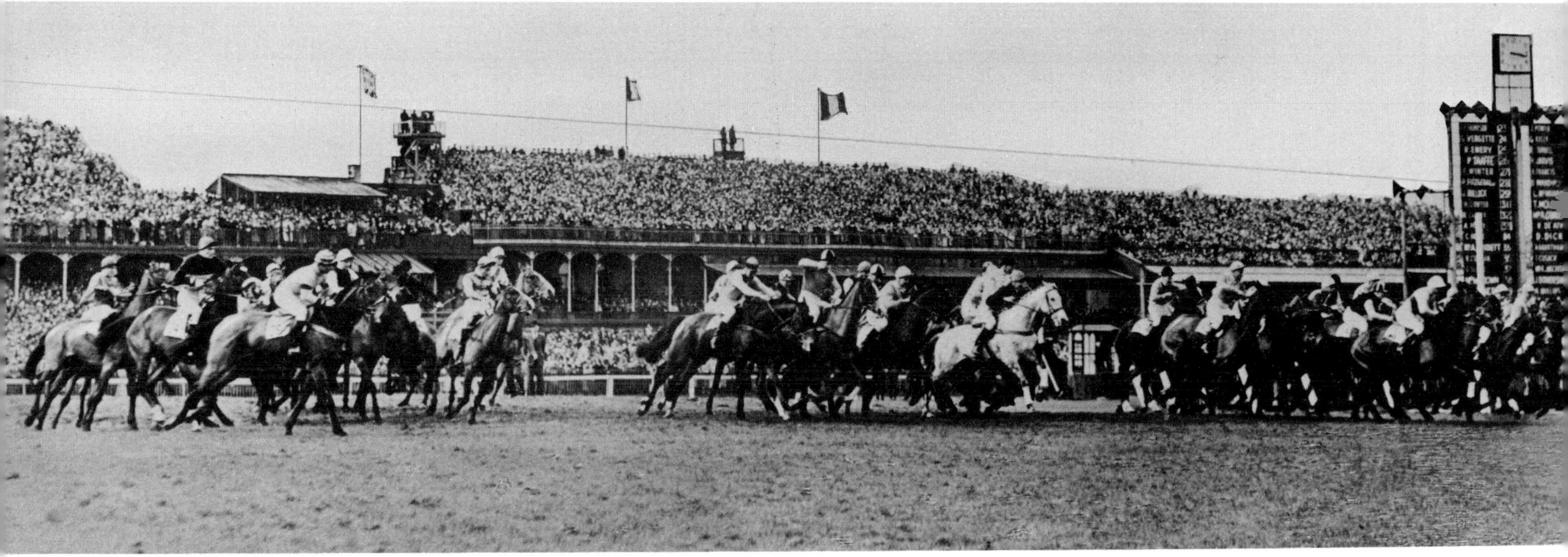

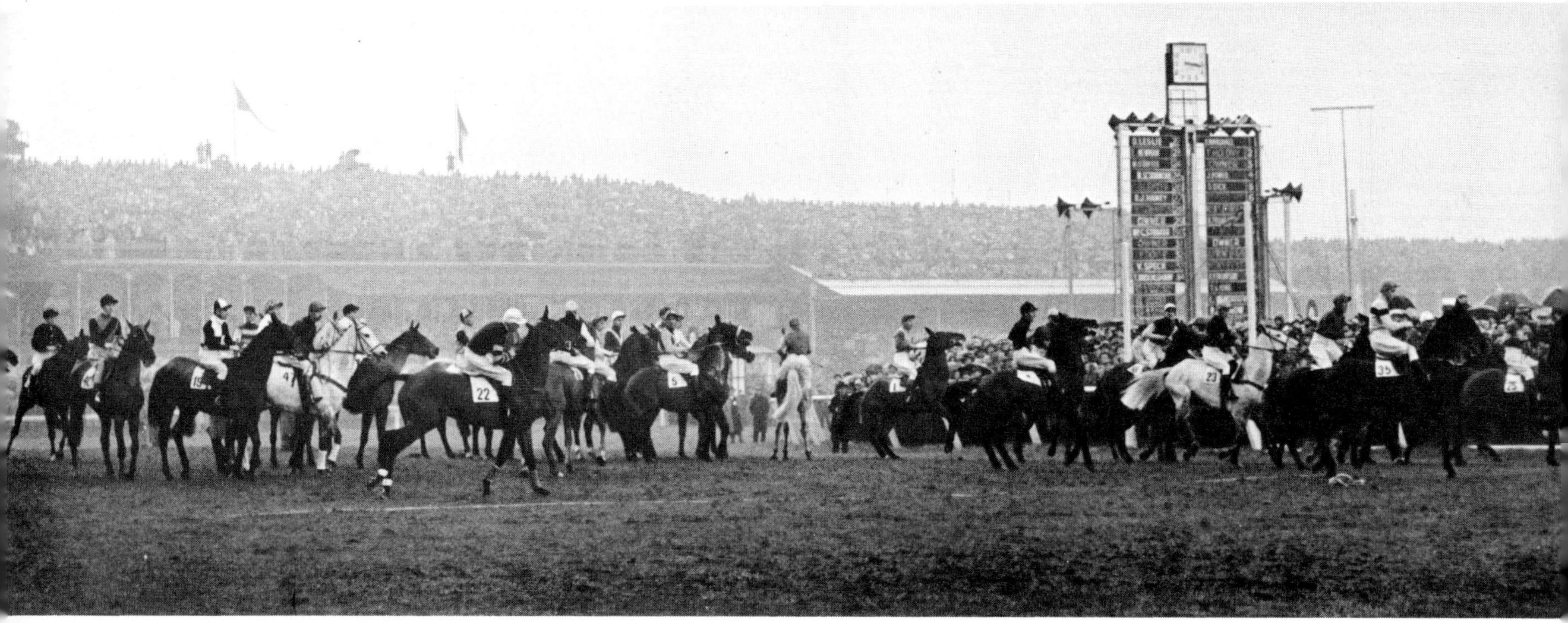

23 The poor Start of 1951.

Theory and Practice 35

and one of three hundred which Aintree has for horses, has housed no less than six National winners in recent years.

Two years after *The Lamb* had won the National in 1868 his rider, Mr. George Ede, who rode as 'Mr. Edwards', was killed when riding in the Sefton 'Chase at Aintree. When the horse came to run in the National of 1871 Lord Poulet had to find another rider. Some time before the race his Lordship had two dreams. In the first *The Lamb* finished last but in the second he won by four lengths and Lord Poulet claimed that he 'saw' not only colours of cerise and blue but also the jockey wearing them— Mr. Tommy Pickernell who rode as 'Mr. Thomas'. The owner wrote to the rider the following day asking him to take the ride and telling him of the two dreams. Pickernell agreed.

On the day of the race a crowd of racegoers arriving at one of the Liverpool stations saw a lamb get loose from a truck in a siding and career about the railway lines.

At Aintree *The Lamb* started second favourite and won easily.

From 1885 until 1907 there used to be a preliminary hurdle on the way to the Start which served to oil the joints of horses and riders alike, and one can easily see the plausibility of having such an obstacle. It was a compulsory jump but did not form part of the course.

In the parade there are always one or two horses out of line 'rarin' to go'. Indeed, the horse which moves quietly in front of these Stands with their electric atmosphere is the exception rather than the rule. Some are just good humoured show-offs playing to the gallery; others are genuinely bursting with energy.

Fifteen minutes from now it will be quite a different story, especially if the going is heavy—which brings up the question of the weather.

1901. The National has never been completely lost to the weather but several years it has been necessary to postpone it and some years this step would have been advisable but was not in fact taken. Such a year was that in which *Grudon* won. The snow was deep enough to cause some of the riders to protest at being asked to ride in such

24 The false Start of 1952.

25 Some of the first fence after effects of the poor Start in 1951 . . .

26 . . . and a few seconds later seen from the opposite side of the course.

conditions which were somewhat enlivened by a severe blizzard, but their objections were overruled. *Grudon's* owner packed the horse's hooves with butter to prevent the snow accumulating and this undoubtedly made the difference between winning and losing. They said that *Grudon* came home 'like a cat through rain' and his time of 9 mins. 47 secs. verifies it. One of the riders said it had been like trying to find the North Pole without a compass.

1911. Ten years later in 1911 the weather had made the underfoot conditions like a glue-pot. The going was so heavy that only *Glenside*, the winner, 'navigated' it successfully and finished alone. *Rathnally*, *Shady Girl* and *Foolhardy* had to be remounted to finish second, third and fourth and these were the only finishers.

1933, 1947. In 1933 the ground rattled when *Kellsboro' Jack* set up a new time record of 9 mins. 28 secs., but in 1947 when *Caughoo* won at 100 to 1 it was on a course which had not only been subjected to snow and frost followed by a thaw and then finally deluged with torrential rain, but one which was shrouded in mist and fog.

1955. In 1955 the course was water-logged in parts especially on the landing side of the Water jump and, ironically, that particular obstacle was omitted. So in 1955 the National had only 29 jumps in its 4 miles 856 yards.

The Start, 1951. The Starter is open to more criticism even than the Handicapper and when in 1951 he inadvertently set the runners off when half of them had their backs to the tape and had made no attempt to get into line, the wrath of everyone descended upon him. The field set off at intervals and the ones who got 'a flyer' went faster than usual in order to take advantage of their lucky break, and the ones 'left' went faster also to try and make up the lost ground. Twelve of the 36 starters either fell or were brought down at the first fence.

1928. The year in which only two finished—1928—it was predicted that there would be chaos at the first fence as there had never been as many runners (42) before.

With this prophesy in mind, *Amberwave*'s jockey held the horse back when the tape went up and gave his 41 opponents a good start. When he reached the fence he discovered there wasn't a faller in sight and the whole field was well on its way to the Second!

The best laid schemes....

Early Speed. In recent years it has become customary for the Senior Steward to address the riders in the Weighing Room before the National warning them against excessive early speed and against crowding over to the inside rails, and these twin causes of many accidents in the past seem to have been curbed.

The First of Thirty. As the first wave of runners reach the first fence and rise in the air together they make an impressive spectacle. But the fence has a psychological attachment to it and, as can be imagined, most riders approach it with apprehension especially if the horse they are riding is making his Aintree debut.

Over the years it has claimed numerous victims—including many star jumpers—*Golden Miller*, for example—so perhaps 'fell at the first' doesn't always mean what it so often derisively implies.

27 1952. After two unsuccessful attempts the runners finally got away but the scene at the first fence was similar to that of 1951.

Theory and Practice 39

The Front-runners. The pace at which the National is run is frequently determined by some tearaway front-runner and how long these horses stay in the race depends upon the extent which their jumping ability can accommodate their impetuosity.

A few years ago *Out and About* lived up to its name for it was always out and about a furlong in front of everything else. Such horses refuse every attempt to settle them down and are by no means easy to ride. Nor are they welcome sights to the riders of other horses as they set a completely false pace and give the field the wrong kind of lead altogether.

The state of the going is also a factor in the shaping of the pace at which the race is run, but the pace is always a fast one in the National.

28 Another view of the first fence in 1952.

Prior to 1961 a field in excess of 25 frequently meant a large number of early fallers and these in turn meant interference. To avoid this hazard those who could made sure that they had as many behind them as possible, and unless a horse was in the leading bunch from the start it was virtually impossible to win the race. Yet this, like every law connected with Aintree, had its exceptions but they were dependent upon a great deal of good fortune in the shape of a clear run. If the old

29 The first open-ditch 1939. Kilstar (23) Dominic's Cross (7) Inversible (14) and Black Hawk (13).

adage 'A person makes his own luck' applied to anything it applied to these circumstances and the wiser ones took notice of it and made sure they were well away from trouble.

1961. But the modification to the fences in 1961 has had several consequences, the chief of which has been the big decrease in the number of fallers on the first circuit, and now probably for the first time since National fields numbered 20 or less it is possible to wait with a horse and not make too much use of him in the early stages.

Tearaways are sometimes brilliant, sometimes carefree but nearly always breathtaking. *Cloister's* impetuous jumping was redeemed by his ability to find an extra leg when it was most needed. *Troytown's* massive frame and strength saw him through his skirmishes with fences. In 1914 the pacemaker, *Sunloch*, showed none of the front-runner's usual reluctance to leave the ground and put in a really bold display of fencing.

The National field of that year included the winner of 1909, *Lutteur III* ridden by Alec Carter and another French hope, *Triannon III* ridden by Charles Hawkins. Both riders had been briefed as to the merits of the other eighteen runners and had been told to disregard the light-weights. Accordingly when the field settled down shortly after the Start and *Sunloch* took up the running they didn't pay a great deal of attention to him for he was carrying a mere 9st. 7lb., and that mostly in the shape of W. J. Smith who was a comparitively inexperienced jockey.

Their lack of concern was obvious when they allowed him to take a lead of first ten, then 20 and finally 40 lengths.

For 24 fences Carter and Hawkins and 17 others offered not the slightest opposition and merely sat with smug beliefs that he would 'come back to them'.

It was not until the Canal Turn on the second circuit that they realized that *Sunloch* wasn't going to come back and they sat down to ride as though Satan himself was on their heels. Although they did narrow the gap *Sunloch* was too far ahead and even though he sprawled on landing at the last fence he was quick to recover and passed the Post an easy winner.

As they come onto the Racecourse. If a horse is not amongst the leaders as they make the Canal Turn on the second circuit it stands very little chance of winning unless the ones ahead of it fall, but in the National anything can happen, and frequently does. Here, more than anywhere, the race is never won until one horse passes the Post.

Invariably the runners are strung out along this last section of the race and from the Anchor Bridge Crossing onwards some horses which have never raced beyond 4 miles find that they can with extremely patient handling manage to get 4½ miles. The horse which truly gets the trip in the National will have made his way to the front as they come onto the racecourse with two fences left, but more than once the National has seemed all over bar the cheering when out of the blue the winner which was imminent resigns and the scene which barely a second ago was a mere formality for one horse now has another hero.

The 29th. In 1936 *Reynoldstown*, the winner of the previous year, was set to carry 12st. 2lb. and looked like defying the burden as he jumped Valentine's on the second circuit just behind *Davy Jones*. At the open ditch after Valentine's, however, he was nearly down and lost quite a lot of ground, but coming on to the racecourse he was narrowing the gap. *Davy Jones* landed over the second last still in the lead and it began to look as though *Reynoldstown* had too much to do.

In order to give himself a few extra inches of rein over the drop fences *Davy Jones'* rider, The Hon. Anthony Mildmay, had decided against tying his reins in the knot which every rider does to avoid putting too much strain on the buckle. Fate wanted no second invitation and as the pin of the buckle shot past the bar the reins flew out of the rider's hands and the horse, with no indication as to direction coming from its helpless rider, ran out before the last.

Reynoldstown, a long way clear of the rest of his field, went on to win his second successive National—the first horse to do so since *The Colonel* in 1869/70.

1928. If any of the 300,000 people (the estimated attendance figures for the time) present at Aintree in 1928 thought they had seen all the drama they were due to see

30 Becher's 1935.

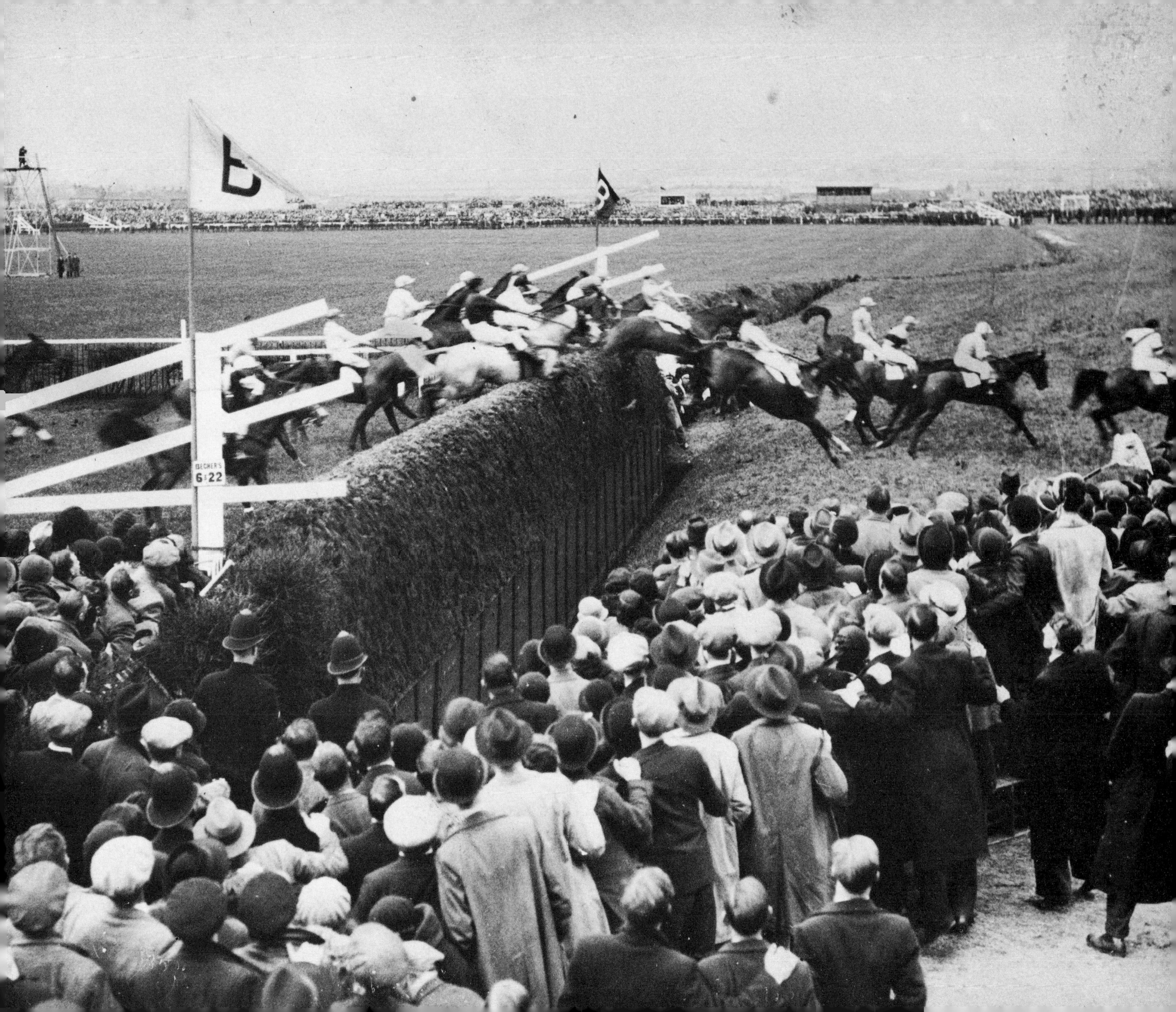
BECHER'S
6 & 22

31 Becher's 1964.

as the six survivors of the Canal Turn fence incident progressed on their way, they were mistaken. The field had included *Sprig*, the 1927 hero, *Bright's Boy* third in 1926, second under 12st. 7lb. in 1927 and *Grakle* who was to win in 1931. The French mare *Maguelonne* was going well when she fell at the fence after Valentine's on the second circuit. This reduced the field to three and left *Great Spann*, ridden by seventeen-year-old Bill Payne, in front as they came onto the racecourse. Close on his heels was *Billy Barton*—a horse which had proved himself the best 'chaser in the U.S.A. The only other horse standing was plodding merrily on in their wake—*Tipperary Tim* ridden by Mr. W. P. Dutton. At the 29th the saddle slipped on *Great Spann* and deposited his rider on the floor. With only one fence to jump *Billy Barton* was being cheered home by the hundreds of Americans in the Stands, but their cheering was premature for *Billy Barton* fell at the last and *Tipperary Tim* and his pilot sailed over it and went on to win one of the most memorable Nationals there has ever been. *Billy Barton* was remounted and finished second and the result of 'only 2 finished' went into the record books for the first time since 1837.

Theory and Practice 45

The 30th. The last fence in the National is the 4 ft 6 in Thorn fence, No. 14 on the first circuit. As already mentioned, in the early years of the race this obstacle was a hurdle. There was a mare called *Fan* which seemed to have an outstanding chance in the National of 1867 and believing that if and when she reached the last hurdle she would be extremely tired someone who stood to gain by her victory sawed through the bar of the hurdle to make it less substantial. *Fan* did reach the obstacle but there was one horse which reached it before her—a very tired *Cortolvin*—and thanks to the sawing operation crashed through it without falling and went on to win. *Fan* was second.

The stories connected with this magical fence are endless. 'If that fence hadn't been there. . . .' Of course, there must be a last fence otherwise National Hunt Racing wouldn't exist.

32 Becher's 1965.

It has a psychological aspect which no other fence has and although it probably presented no problems on the first circuit it takes on fantastic dimensions as the runners come to it now, on the second circuit.

A rider's attitude may be full of caution on the one hand and carefree abandon on the other. The cautious seem to put *themselves* to the fence rather than the horse, whereas the others seem to ride at it as though it didn't exist. One rider would gladly get off and lift his mount over if he could, whilst another kicks merrily into it as though it was the second or the fourth or the fourteenth.

But whichever type he is the rider who approaches the last fence in the National with a chance gets a clear if distant view of the Winning Post. With what he has gone either through or over during the last ten minutes or so still fresh in his mind, is there any wonder that the butterflies which he thought he had got rid of after the start should now return?

1948. Aintree has witnessed horses running out at the last and horses falling at the last, and once saw a rider take the wrong course as he approached the last. The rider concerned in this last instance was Eddie Reavey and on the morning of the race he had walked the course but for some reason he got a wrong impression of the route to be taken in missing out the Chair on the second circuit, and in the race he in fact missed out the last. He was riding a horse called *First of the Dandies* and considered himself certain to have won as the horse was 'only cantering' when it happened.

The roar of the crowd. As the leading horse jumps the last fence the roar of the crowd is deafening. This is one time when the racegoer doesn't allow his pocket to interfere with his appreciation of a winner, but the roar has to be deafening before either horse or rider hears it for they are travelling at a different speed.

Heart-break Hill. The run-in skirts round 'The Chair' and the Water jump and the ground rises gradually to the Winning Post. Some years ago there was a good Irish mare whose name *Heartbreak Hill* was an apt description of these 494 yards which separate the last fence from the Winning Post. If a horse has a claim to stamina this

33 The first Canal Turn 1930.

34 The first Canal Turn 1966. April Rose (23) Flying Wild (4) Blackspot (46) Stirling (5).

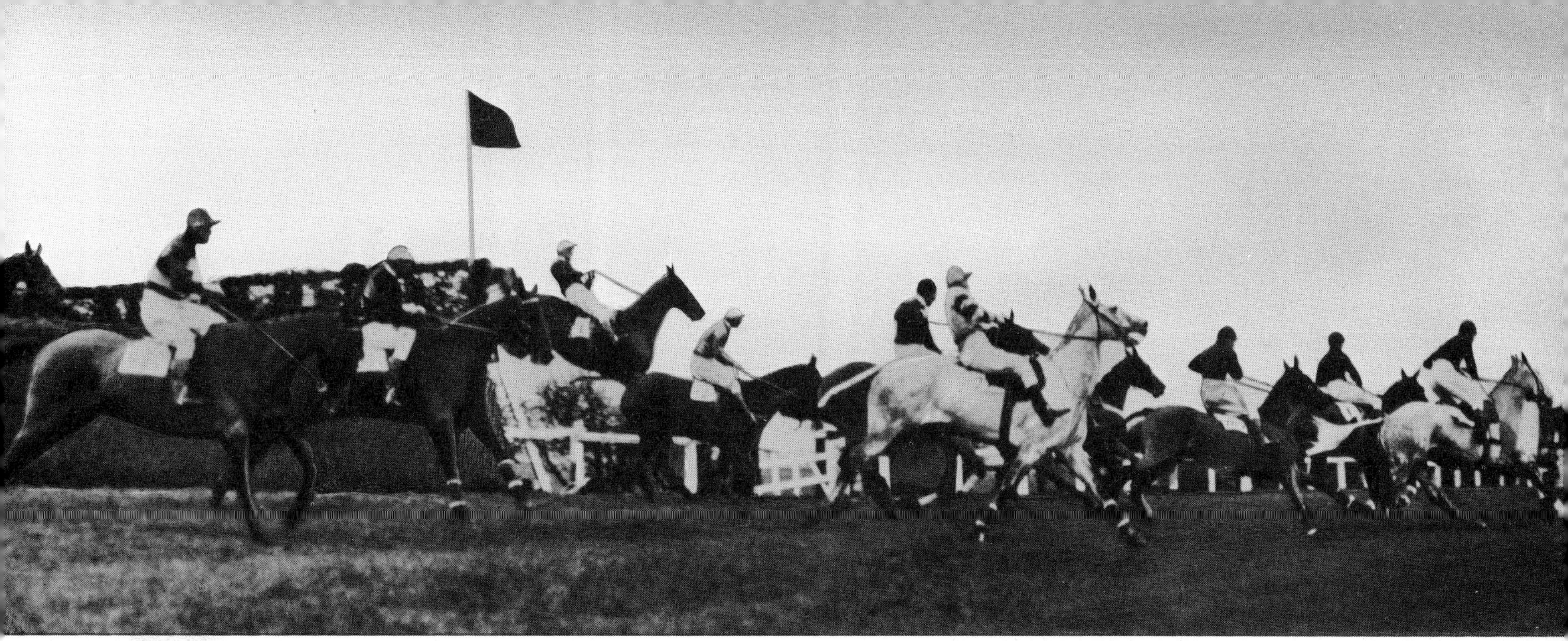

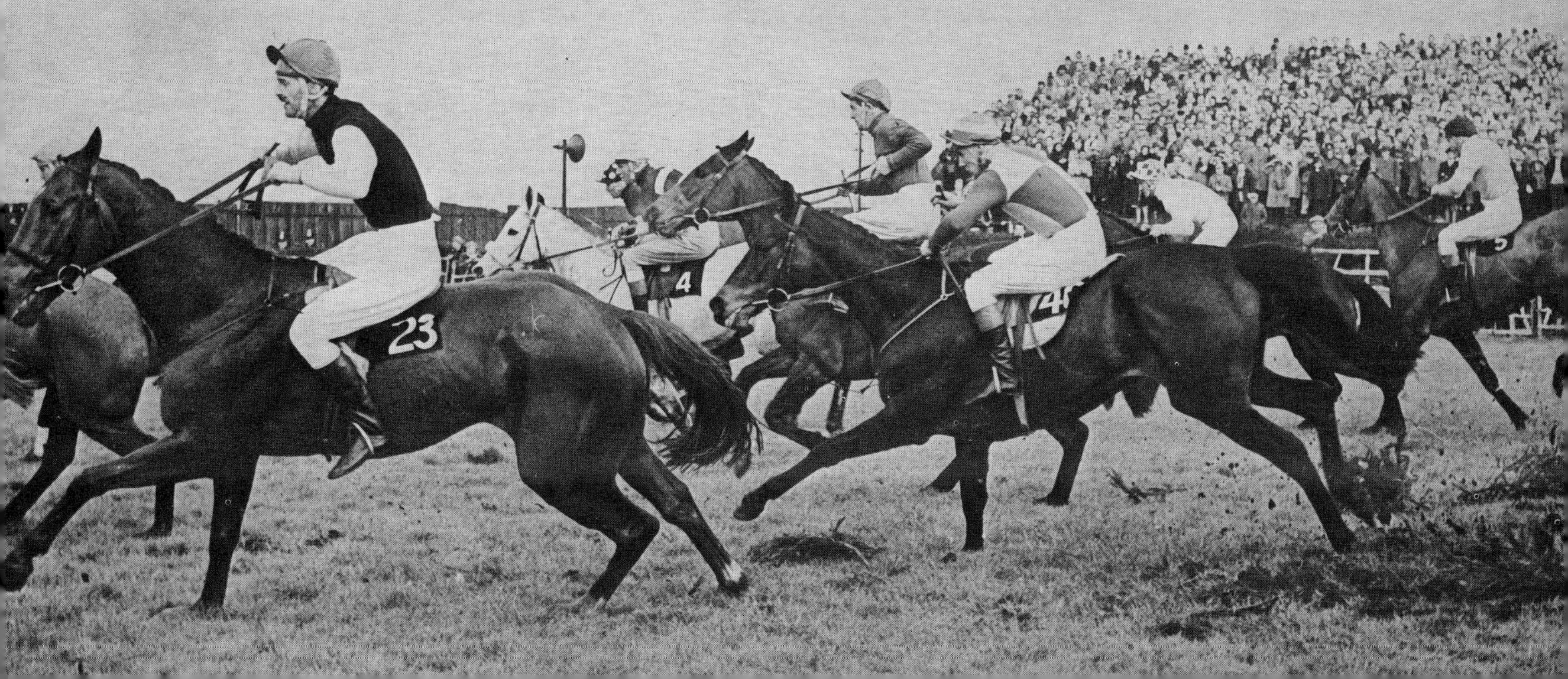
23
4

is where he must prove it, for every pound on his back at this point will count as two or, if the going is heavy, as much as three.

So many times has it been said: 'As long as there were fences to jump he was the

35 *The Canal Turn Fence* 1953.

winner. . . .' But this heart-breaking stretch of ground is very often the undoing of many a horse 'there with a chance' as it jumps the last. Seemingly full of running they have soon been drained of all reserves on this infamous stretch of ground which is so bare of obstacles and their riders have experienced in broad daylight that classical nightmare situation in which the harder one tries to run the more one seems glued to the spot.

1963 and 1964. John Lawrence had this experience on *Carrickbeg*. He passed *Ayala* about half-way up the run-in and Pat Buckley, *Ayala's* rider shouted encouragement. Fifty yards from home *Carrickbeg* was a spent force and Pat Buckley rallied *Ayala* to come again and pass *Carrickbeg* and snatch the verdict. The following year *Team Spirit* won the same way—just getting up to beat *Purple Silk* by half a length.

1938 Battleship. The year 1938 saw another thrilling National. At the second Becher's *Battleship*, a little 15·2 entire horse, and the magnificent *Royal Danieli* led from *Workman* by about five or six lengths. Three out *Battleship* made a mistake and *Workman* passed him into second place. At the next fence *Workman* blundered and *Battleship* took second place to *Royal Danieli*. As they started the long run-in the smaller horse was two lengths in arrears but ridden only with hands and heels he steadily gained on his opponent until a few strides from the Post they were level. After they had gone past the Post the seconds ticked by in silence as the crowd waited for the Judge's verdict. When *Battleship's* number went in the frame the biggest cheers came from the Bookmakers for the little horse had won at 40–1. It had been a subject for a photograph finish but at Aintree the Judge's view has never been aided by a camera to this day, and even though there have been several very close finishes there has never been a dead heat for the National, yet there have been times when it has been said that it was impossible to separate two finishers. Many of those present on the Stands in 1954 found it hard to say immediately which horse had won even though they had just witnessed the finish of the race, and if the finishes of some Nationals have lacked the excitement of cliff-hangers the race in 1954 had more than its share.

1954 Royal Tan. *Royal Tan* had lost a National through a last fence blunder in 1951. At the same fence in 1952 he fell when he would otherwise have finished second to *Teal*. Since then he had been fired and given a year's rest and was now back again —a new horse. Bryan Marshall was riding him thus providing the same combination of owner, trainer and jockey which had been successful the year previously. The second horse in the 1953 National, *Tudor Line*, was there in the line-up again and *Royal Tan's* stable had a well fancied second string in *Churchtown* ridden by Toss Taaffe.

There had been three fatal accidents already when, three fences out, *Conneyburrow* became the fourth. Coming to the second last *Churchtown*, *Tudor Line* and *Royal Tan* were the three leaders. At this fence *Churchtown* blundered and between the last two *Royal Tan* took up the running. *Tudor Line* had jumped to the right at each of the four previous fences and did so again at the last. As *Royal Tan* approached his bogey fence there was a hushed silence but he brushed aside the question mark and scarcely had he got a foot on the ground than Bryan Marshall was driving him home for all he was worth. He poached a lead of a couple of lengths on *Tudor Line* but as they pulled away from *Irish Lizard*, the favourite, who had run on into third place, *Tudor Line* was winning back those two lengths. Three hundred yards out as they passed The Chair fence only a length separated them. As they were opposite the Water *Tudor Line* had only half a length to find and was receiving a stone from his rival, but brilliant riding by Bryan Marshall almost lifted *Royal Tan* past the Post still a neck to the good. Three weeks prior to the race Marshall had fractured his jaw in five places and was told by a Specialist that he was asking for trouble by riding anywhere, let alone in the National.

Royal Tan's win under 11st. 7lb. on going which was officially described as 'yielding' makes his time of 9 mins. $32\frac{4}{5}$ secs. a good one.

But not all Nationals have been so closely contested.

After four gruelling miles and thirty fences the brilliant *Troytown* lengthened his stride to come away from the last and he was starting another circuit before Jack Anthony could pull him up. *Moifaa* was a similar kind of winner and was approaching the first fence again before he could be slowed to a walk. When *Cloister* won in 1893

36 The Chair Fence 1961. Imposant, the leader, Scottish Flight partly hidden and Tonjo and Merryman II (with sash) jumping the fence.

37 The Water 1951. Nickel Coin, Derrinstown (33) and Royal Tan.

38 1955—The year they missed the Water jump out.

he carried 12st. 7lb. the first horse ever to do so and was 40 lengths clear of the second horse.

Salamander (1866) carrying 10st. 7lb. won the race pulling up by 10 lengths from *Cortolvin*, the 1867 winner. *Eremon's* performance in winning the National of 1907 with 10st. 1lb. was a lot easier than the winning margin of six lengths suggests for Alfred Newey who rode him lost an iron at the second fence and was not able to give the horse very much assistance thereafter, but he was at one stage twenty lengths in front of the rest of the runners. There have been years when the rising ground of the run-in has suited a horse perfectly as in 1925. *Double Chance* was lying only third to *Old Tay Bridge* and *Fly Mask* as they jumped the last but sprinted away to win on the run-in.

However, the range from 'with obvious ease' to 'under extreme distress' is sometimes not all that wide and the one becomes the other in almost as short a time as it has taken to write this sentence.

1956 Devon Loch and E.S.B. Throughout the 1956 Grand National Her Majesty the Queen Mother's *Devon Loch*, ridden by Dick Francis, had been virtually foot perfect. He jumped the last fence in the lead from *E.S.B.* and on the run-in he began to draw away from the other horse. Dave Dick, *E.S.B.'s* rider, dropped his hands and settled for second place.

Then, suddenly, and without warning, *Devon Loch's* legs splayed out under him. Subsequent explanations were numerous—that he jumped the shadow of the Water jump, that it was caused by cramp, that he had a heart attack, etc. Dick Francis, the Royal jockey, thought that it was the deafening roar of the crowd at the anticipated victory of the Queen Mother's horse. This last seems feasible for when muscles have been strained in concentrated effort for such a length of time the first sign of relaxing that concentration and nervous strain and they become like jelly.

The roar of the Aintree crowd at the sight of the Royal horse about to win the National could have been loud enough to distract the horse's attention, and perhaps the excitement, so expressed, was the very thing which robbed the owner and the public of the sight they most wanted to see.

39 The Water 1956

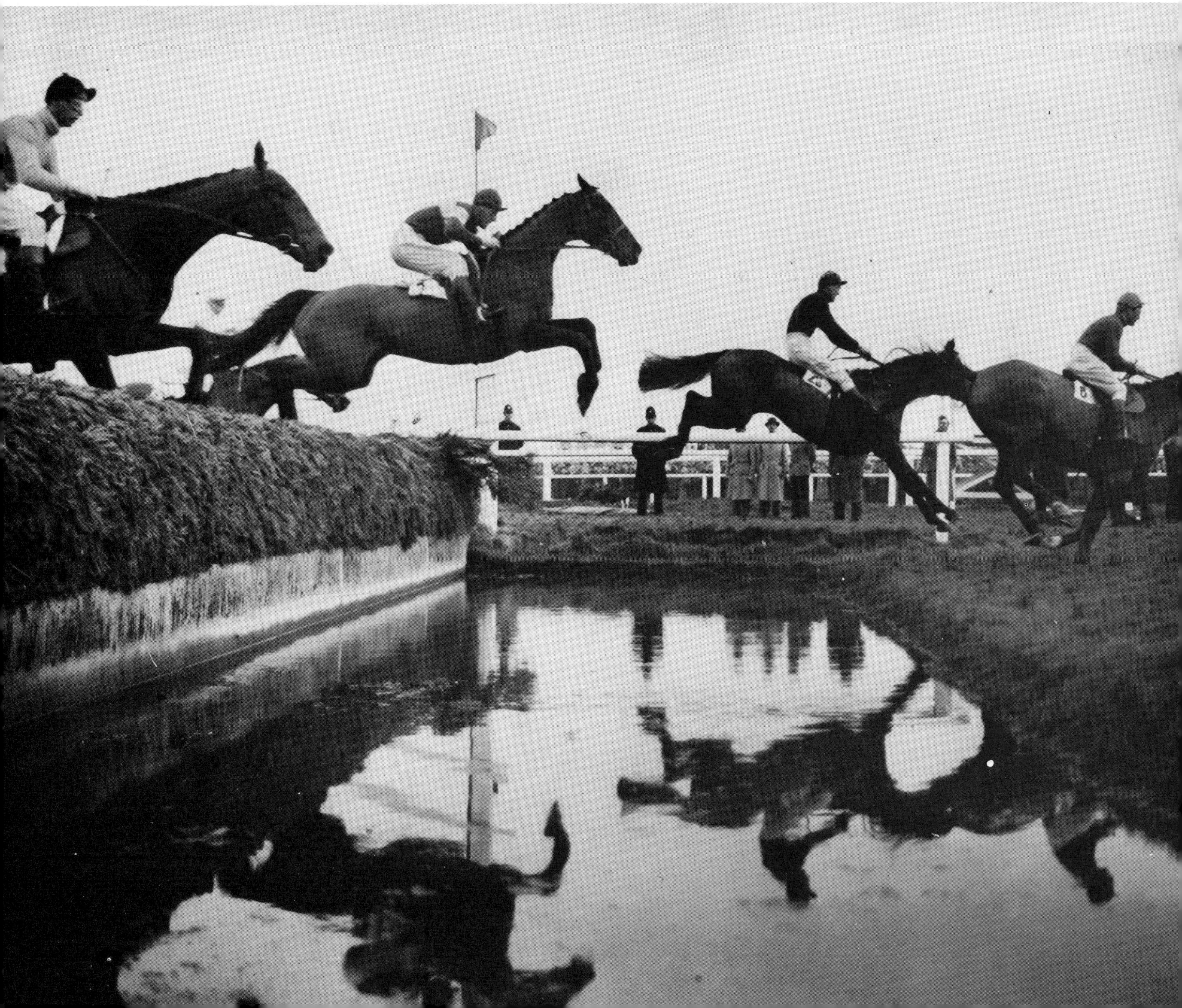

Whatever the cause the horse was up on his feet again in a second but *E.S.B.* had gone on to win and Dick Francis led *Devon Loch* back. Subsequent veterinary examination could find nothing amiss. Had the horse completed the race without this misfortune he would have undoubtedly lowered the record for the fastest time for the National as *E.S.B.'s* time was only one second slower than *Golden Miller's* time of 9 mins. 20$\frac{2}{5}$ secs.

The following day the distance from the point where *Devon Loch* fell to the Winning Post was measured and found to be just 56 yards.

The Loose Horse. When Shakespeare wrote:

> Broad breast, full eye, small head and nostril wide,
> High crest, short ears, straight legs and passing strong,
> Thin mane, thick tail, broad buttock, tender hide,
> Look, what a horse should have he did not lack,
> Save a proud rider on so proud a back.

he unquestionably had in mind the loose horse at Aintree.

This phenomenon, which appears in greater numbers at Liverpool than elsewhere, makes his debut at any stage after the first fence. He comes from that group of horses which unship their riders rather than fall with them and they seem to perform the act with the nonchalant ease of magicians, hardly losing their positions in the field in the process.

National Disasters. The loose horse's appearance on the scene in the middle stages of the National invariably takes the following pattern.

Having got to the head of the field and acquired a lead of some two or three lengths he will gallop on in the most resolute fashion. Once within thirty yards of the fence he enters that psychological danger zone which is typified by the person who has climbed up to the highest diving board and dithers there not sure whether he dare go through with it and yet not having the courage to climb down.

The loose horse will look everything a horse should look as it approaches a fence. The ears will be pricked, the nostrils flared, the stride will shorten slightly as he

Theory and Practice 55

measures the fence and then at the very last second as though someone had whispered in his ear 'It's a drop fence', he will sheer off to the right or left and run across the face of the fence just in time to collide with the first of the oncoming horses.

1967. This is exactly what happened in 1967 at the 23rd fence when, of the 27 horses remaining in the race from an original field of 44, all were involved in a pile-up with

40 At the end of the first circuit 1948.

the exception of one. The scene resembled a battlefield; the fence was demolished, and riders were trying to find their horses and the horses were trying to escape from the melee; the race had to come to a halt and it was hard to tell in which direction the runners had been going before the incident, for there were as many riders and jockeys on one side of what was the fence as there were on the other. Only the wings of the fence were any indication of direction. But one horse got through all this—*Foinavon*—and set up an unassailable lead to win as he pleased.

1928. Whilst they do not rank as annual events pile-ups such as that of 1967 have happened in other Nationals. In 1928 the fiasco which *Amberwave's* jockey expected would occur at the first fence did in fact take place at the Canal Turn fence which at that time was an open ditch. *Easter Hero*, the horse which was to win the Gold Cup in 1929 and run second in the National of that year either took off too soon or made a half-hearted attempt to jump the fence. His effort landed him on top of the fence and then he slipped back into the ditch and baulked all but about six of the rest of the field.

The escalating nature of the havoc caused by a loose horse in the middle stages of the National tends to cover his original guilt, but the loose horse matching strides in the closing stages with a horse which has obviously a great chance of winning the race is right in the limelight and his behaviour is there for all the world to see. The longer he remains upsides the other horse the more the tension grows as every witness of the drama will know, for the possibility of the loose horse jumping across the other one or carrying it out is very real and increases with every stride.

1946. In 1946 *Prince Regent*, ridden by Tim Hyde, was carrying 12st. 5lb. and at Valentine's the second time he went into the lead. But from the 27th fence onwards he was continually baulked by a loose horse. Capt. Bobby Petre, who rode the winner, *Lovely Cottage*, said afterwards that Hyde had been forced to ride the equivalent of a finish approaching each of the last three fences to avoid interference from the riderless horse, and it can be imagined how much this must have been the cause of *Prince Regent* starting the gruelling run-in already a spent force.

5. Chance and Coincidence

The history of the Grand National is full of events and situations which, had they been invented by the novelist or playwright, would have been rejected as being too outlandish to be possible.

Emigrant 1857. Two years before he won the National *Emigrant* had been owned by the well known trainer Ben Land, but he changed hands in circumstances which, if not unique, were at least unusual. Land was staying at the George Hotel in Shrewsbury and one night was losing at cards. To cover his losses he sold *Emigrant* to another trainer—Hodgman, for £590. In 1856 *Emigrant* was unsuccessful in his first attempt to win the National but the following year his weight had been reduced from 10st. 2lb. to 9st. 12lb. and Hodgman engaged Charles Boyce to ride. A week before the race Boyce badly injured his arm in a hunting accident. Hodgman's opinion of Boyce's ability was so high that in spite of his injury the rider took his place on *Emigrant* in the line-up with his arm strapped to his side. Hodgman backed *Emigrant* not only to win £25,000 but to be first over the Water. *Emigrant* reached the jump just a stride behind *Westminster* but Hodgman's wager was safe for *Emigrant* was such a quick jumper that although he took off after *Westminster* he landed before him.

Along the Canal there was a patch of very heavy going and Boyce switched *Emigrant* to the ground alongside the towpath and to do this he had to jump a small fence. The Conditions of Entry stated 'no rider to open a gate or ride through a gateway; or more than 100 yards along any road, footpath or driftway'. Boyce had done none of these things and so he was in the clear, and whilst his opponents ploughed through the heavy going *Emigrant* conserved his energy. However, at the last he was joined by *Weathercock*, but the good ride which Boyce had given him enabled *Emigrant* to draw away and win by an easy two lengths.

The owner-trainer of *Weathercock* was none other than Ben Land.

Seaman 1882. In 1881 Lord Manners, a young Guards Officer, was looking for a horse to ride in the National. Not unnaturally his search led him to Ireland to Linde's establishment at Eyrefield Lodge, for Linde had trained the winners of the

41 The first Valentine's 1926. Darrack leads the eventual winner, Jack Horner. Lord Sefton's Stand is in the background.

42 The 27th in 1927. Sprig (No. 4) the winner, Bright's Boy (No. 1) was third.

two previous Nationals (*Empress* 1880 and *Woodbrook* 1881). Amongst many others there was a horse with exceptional ability called *Seaman* whose victories included the Paris Hurdle and Conyngham Cup at Punchestown. Locally it was believed that the horse would not stand training because of a doubtful leg but Lord Manners was unaware of this and offered £2,000 for *Seaman*. Horse coping was part of Linde's trade and he persuaded the horse's owner, John Gubbins, to accept the offer.

The legal aspect of the sale of an unsound horse placed the onus on the purchaser in view of the fact that Lord Manners had approached Linde with his offer. Had Linde offered the horse for sale it would have been his duty to declare all the facts. The sequence of events, however, was governed by the principle of 'caveat emptor'—'let the buyer beware'.

Lord Manners sent his new acquisition to be trained at Newmarket by James Jewitt who controlled Capt. Machell's horses. The Captain had already had three National winners in *Disturbance*, *Reugny* and *Regal* and did not have a very high opinion of Lord Manners' recent purchase, nor of its prospects of winning the National with his Lordship in the saddle. Jewitt gave the horse as much work as he dare in the circumstances and despatched him to Liverpool along with his other runner, *The Scott*, which he was to ride himself.

On the day of the race the first and second favourites were *Mohican* and *Cyrus*—both trained by Linde, with Mr. Tommy Beasley (who had ridden *Empress* and *Woodbrook* to victory) on *Cyrus*. The weather was inclement to say the least and snow

43–5 Grifel, the Russian horse, falls at Becher's on the first circuit in 1961. He was remounted but finally refused at the 19th.

Chance and Coincidence 61

smarted on the faces of the riders in the parade. Capt. Machell advised Lord Manners to tie a knot in his reins and leave the rest to *Seaman*, for it was no understatement to say that his Lordship's experience of riding in public against such able men as Tommy Beasley and the other leading National Hunt riders had been limited.

Zoedone, who was to win the race the following year, led the field onto the racecourse on the second circuit but was beaten at that point. At the last *Seaman* had made his way through the others to be only a length behind *Cyrus*. Even then his prospects seemed slight for Beasley's greater experience in riding a finish was sure to be the decisive factor. However, inch by inch Lord Manners and *Seaman* lessened the gap and by the time they passed the Post they were a head in front. Lord Manners'

46 Becher's on the first circuit 1955.

62 *Chance and Coincidence*

47 1930. May King falls at Becher's.

48 Red Alligator (22), the winner, jumps over the fallen Polaris Missile at Becher's on the first circuit 1968.

Chance and Coincidence 63

49 1923. Trentino falls at Becher's.

50 The second Becher's 1970. Villay (31) leads Miss Hunter (23) and Gay Trip (2) the winner.

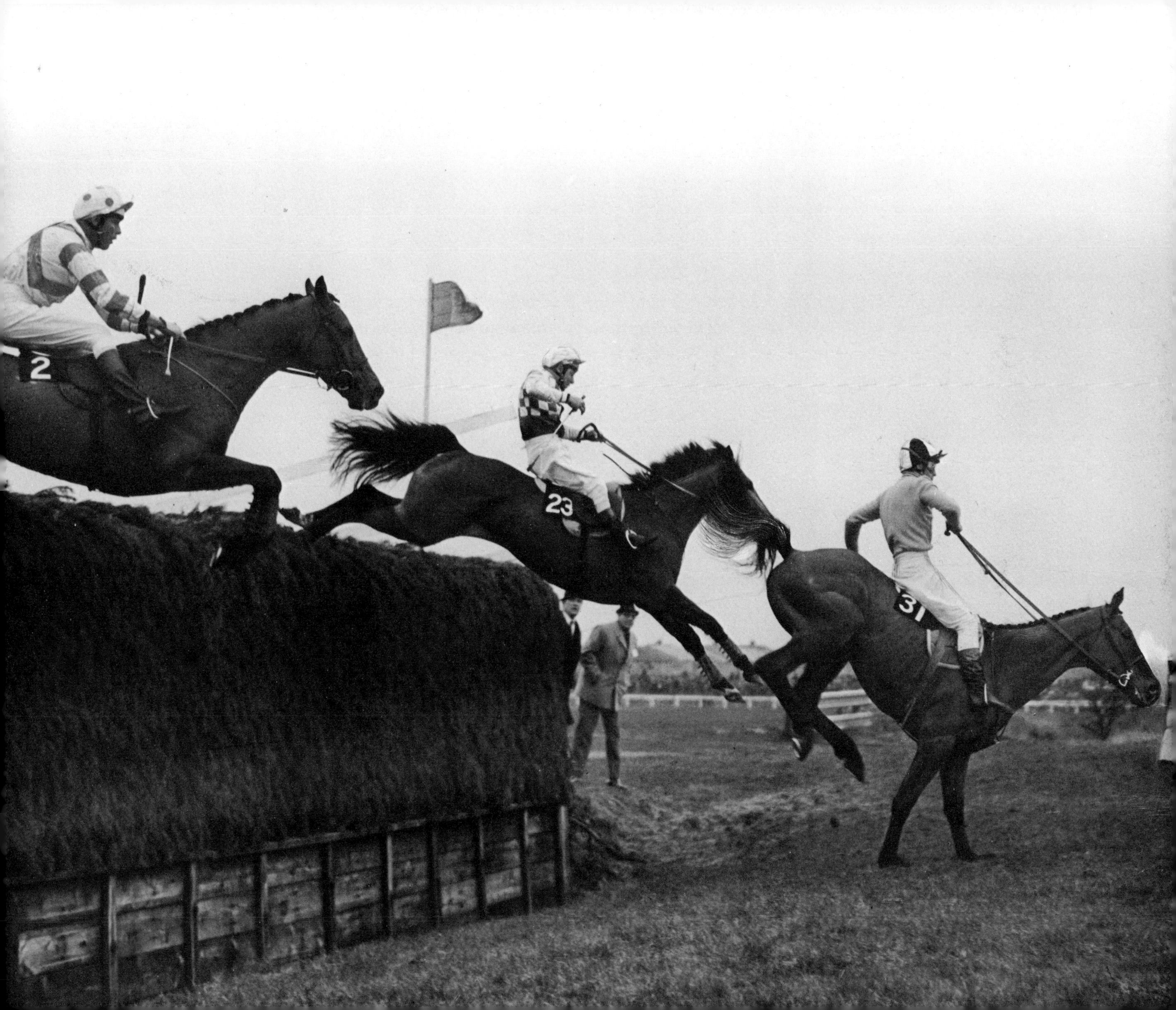
2
23
31

hands were raw but he still held onto the knot which Capt. Machell had advised him to tie.

Cyrus was owned by John Gubbins.

Seaman had broken down at the last and Lord Manners never ran him again. He became the family favourite and enjoyed his retirement.

Sundew 1956. Mrs. G. Kohn had sold her share in *E.S.B.* before he won the National in 1956. She owned another horse called *Sundew* but he had fallen in both his attempts at the National—once at the 28th and once at the 22nd. It was thought that he did not stay the distance. He was ten years old in 1956 and in view of his limitations he was sent up to the Sales but, strangely, he did not attract a bid. Subsequently, Mrs. Kohn tried to sell him privately but without success and so reluctantly he was put back into training. Having survived all her efforts to sell him he fulfilled Mrs. Kohn's ambitions by winning the National for her in 1957 at his third attempt, and he was the first of Fred Winter's two National winners as a rider.

The year after he won the National *Sundew* fell at The Water jump at Haydock Park and broke his back and he is buried on the course.

Romantic stories of Grand National winners pulling ploughs or carts prior to winning the big race or changing hands for a few pounds do have some origin in fact.

Chandler 1848. *Chandler* did once pull a chandler's cart. He was sold to a man who used to drive him in a gig to the Hunt. One day Captain Peel—a famous amateur rider—was waiting for his own horse to be brought to the Meet when the owner of *Chandler* offered to lend him to Capt. Peel. By coincidence there was a bridle and saddle in the gig and Capt. Peel had such a fine ride from *Chandler* that on his return he offered the horse's owner 20 guineas plus his (Capt. Peel's) own horse which had now turned up, in exchange for *Chandler*. The deal was done. Several days later Capt. Peel received his own horse back and this he sold for 60 guineas, so in actual fact he bought *Chandler* for 20 guineas. For the next five years *Chandler* was hunted and then tried in a Steeplechase at Birmingham in which he finished second. Warwick was the

51 Flying Wild (No. 4) and Pat Taaffe make a determined effort to avoid Game Purston's fallen jockey Paddy Cowley.

52 1966. The Japanese horse Fujino-O is led from the ditch at the Chair fence as Jeff King, his jockey, steps back to course-level.

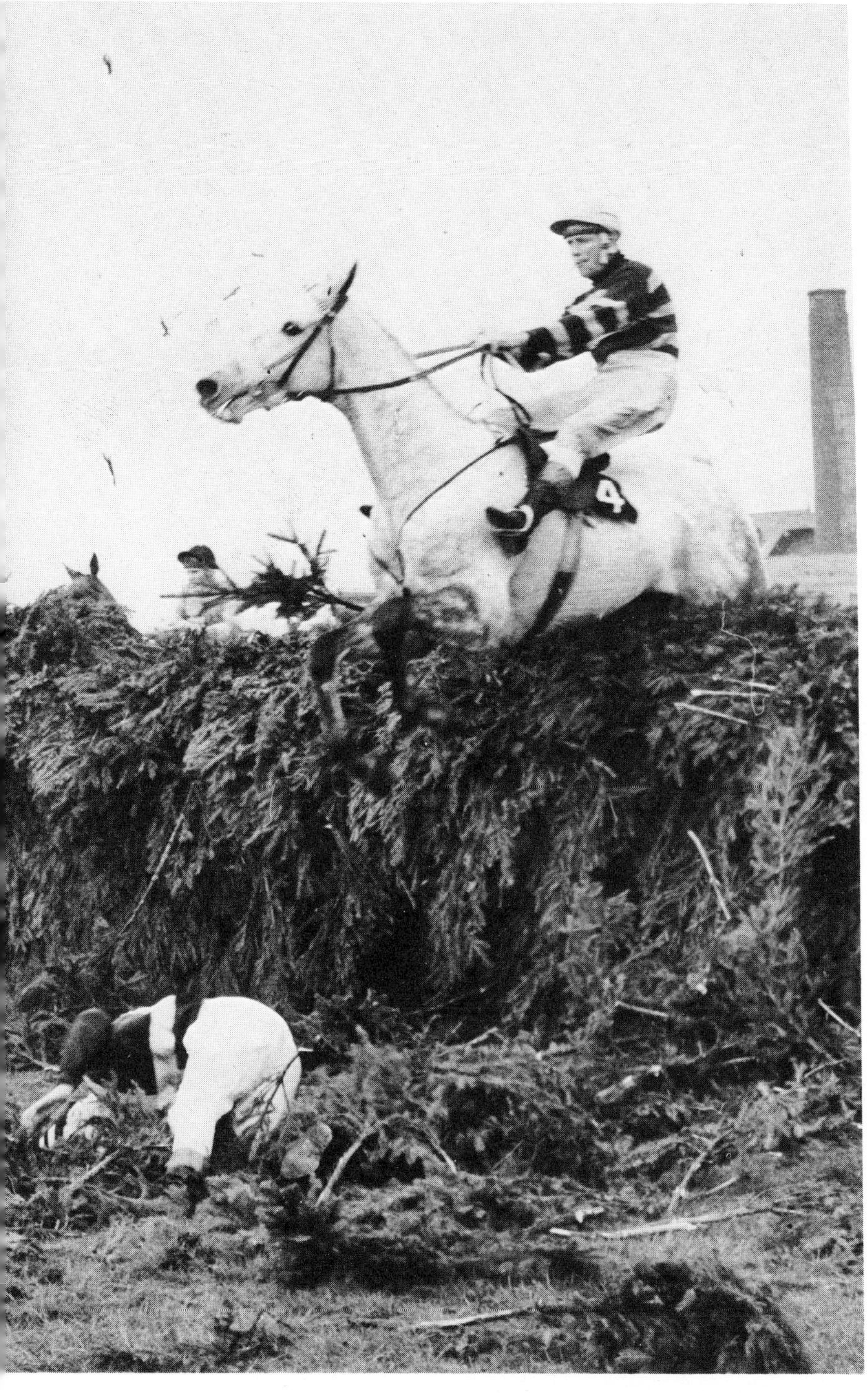
4

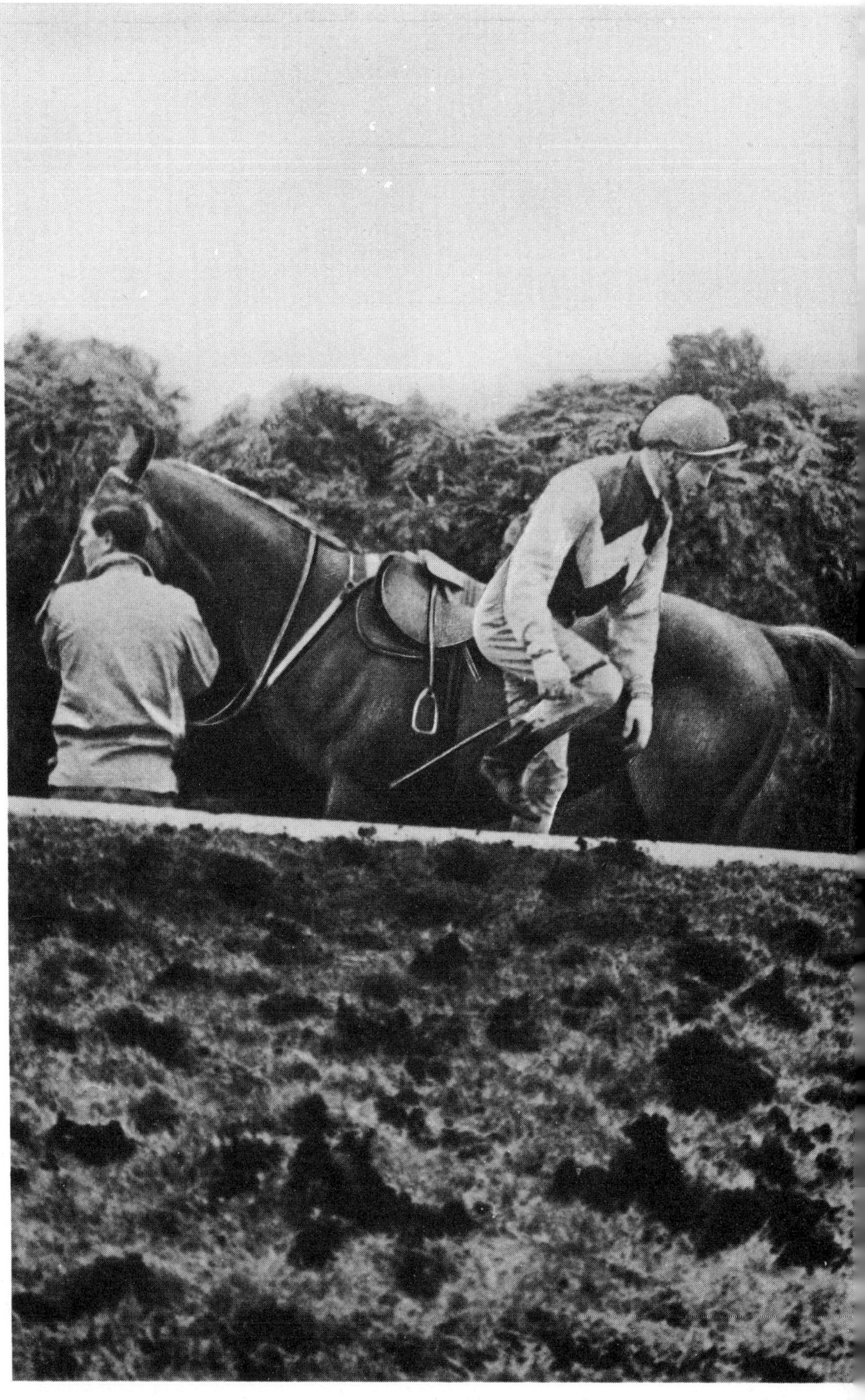

53 The 23rd fence 1967. The race comes to a halt. Foinavon can be seen jumping the remains of the fence on the top right of the picture.

54 The 23rd fence 1967. Most of the runners re-assembled.

55 The 23rd fence 1967. The last few to get away again.

56 The last fence 1928—from left to right, Tipperary Tim the riderless Great Span and Billy Barton the American horse whose compatriots had started to cheer him home, but a second later he fell and Tipperary Tim came home alone. Billy Barton was remounted and was the only other horse to finish from 42 starters.

57 The last fence 1951. Royal Tan blunders his chance away and Nickel Coin went on to win.

venue of his next race which he won by 20 lengths, and at the last fence it is claimed he jumped thirty-seven feet.

Subsequently Captain 'Josey' Little bought a half share in him and rode him in the National of 1848 which they won.

Rubio 1908. *Rubio*, the National winner of 1908, was bought for 15 guineas as a yearling. He was an American bred horse and was bought by Major Douglas-Pennant in the hope that he would make a hunter. He was turned out until he was rising four and then hunted. Put into training as a five-year-old he won three races before he broke down. His owner then lent him to the landlord of The Prospect Arms at Towcester to run him in harness pulling the station omnibus in the hope that the road work would make his legs sound again. It did and three years later he was back in training. In 1907 he won two races and in 1908 he won the National.

Salamander was bought by Mr. Edward Studd for £35 and won the National in 1866. The same man refused *The Lamb* at £30 with words to the effect that the horse was not worthy to carry a man's boots let alone a man. When *The Lamb* won the second of his two Grand Nationals the horse which was runner-up to him was called *Despatch* and was owned by none other than Edward Studd.

Master Robert 1924. The ex-plough horse was in fact *Master Robert*. He was bred by Mr. R. McKinley and put into training but he was judged too slow for racing and returned to Mr. McKinley's farm. Being a big horse his owner kept him employed in the plough until selling him for £50. He ultimately passed into the ownership of Lord Airlie and Mr. Sidney Green and they sent him to be trained by Aubrey Hastings. It was discovered that the horse had a diseased bone in his foot and was put under the expert care of Frank Cundell, the Veterinary Surgeon. Road work was the cure as it had been with *Rubio*, but in the early stages constant poulticing was necessary to give the horse relief.

He recovered sufficiently well to stand training but the foot was never fully sound and, in fact, a few days before he won the National in 1924 he ran at Wolverhampton and pulled up lame.

58 The Devon Loch drama of 1956.

59 The Devon Loch drama of 1956.

Bob Trudgill, a tough rider whose tally of falls from bad horses was countless, was engaged to ride him in the National and the day previous to the race took another bad fall from a horse called *Charlie Wise*. He was determined to ride *Master Robert* though, and ride he did, to win by four lengths from *Fly Mask* with *Silvo*—the horse which had been bought for 10,500 guineas—third. Trudgill collapsed in the Weighing Room but managed to weigh in.

Whereas *Rubio* had cost 15 guineas and *Master Robert* £50, *Double Chance*, the 1925 winner, was given by Mr. Anthony de Rothschild to Frederick Archer (a nephew of the renowned Fred Archer) because the horse was unsound. Archer hunted him, fired him, rested him and then won five small races with him before training him to win the National.

6.
National Heroes

'So did this horse excel a common one
In shape, in courage, colour, pace and bone'.

VENUS AND ADONIS

After the winner has been unsaddled and the 'weighed-in' flag hoisted there follows that little ceremony of placing the Blue Riband round the neck of the winner.

When The Hon. Geo. Lambton wrote to the Press concerning the weight range of the handicap he started with the words: 'The Grand National is the Blue Riband of Steeplechasing, it is not meant to be won by a moderate horse'.

A moderate horse could not win the Grand National. Success in this marathon steeplechase shows an ability which no moderate horse could produce, and even a National winner with form which was moderate prior to winning the race is certainly not a moderate horse on the day he passes the Post first at Liverpool, even should he fail to reproduce the form subsequently. The stiffness of the course ensures this much.

Whilst between themselves all National winners are equal, like the inhabitants of 'Animal Farm', some are more equal than others. Comparison of National winners is a difficult undertaking. The differences in the length of the courses prior to 1885 (or thereabouts) plus the different surfaces (some with more plough than others) over which they raced and the variations to the fences, not to mention the changes in the going (as an after effect of the weather)—all these things make it difficult to do more than appreciate each National winner for its own sake.

Perhaps the furthest one can go in this respect is to say that some National winners have a status which is relative to the particular National they won, others were outstanding in a decade or so and yet a third group were individually brilliant against the background of the complete history of the race.

Lottery 1839. In order of time the first of these heroes was the 'cocktail' horse *Lottery*.

Originally he was called *Chance* and was by another horse called *Lottery*. He was bought by John Elmore at Horncastle Fair for either one hundred and twenty or one hundred and eighty guineas at a time when the cocktail or part-bred hunter was almost itself a form of currency in some quarters.

He won races everywhere including the famous National of 1839, and as his prowess grew Racecourse Executives framed their Entry Conditions 'Open to all horses except *Lottery*', or, '10 sovs. each but *Lottery* 40 sov'. Even Liverpool imposed a penalty of 18lb. 'to be carried by the winner of The Cheltenham Steeplechase' which, of course, was *Lottery*, and consequently he went to Post in 1840 with the impossible weight of 13st. 4lb.

Throughout his career he was ridden by 'Jem' Mason and the partnership was known throughout the land, but in spite of these successes *Lottery* hated the sight of Mason and it was necessary to resort to all manner of tricks in order to get Mason into the saddle. Once there, however, the horse accepted the situation and got on with his job.

In a race at Dunchurch he was so far in front of the rest of the field that Mason allowed him to trot over some ploughland. Alan McDonough, the famous Irish rider, who had ridden in the race said that *Lottery* must 'surely be the best horse in the world, for he could trot faster than any of the rest of us could gallop'.

The four dual-National winners, *Abd-el-Kader*, *Peter Simple*,* *The Colonel* and *The Lamb*, together with *Emigrant* and *Salamander*, were the best winners between 1849 and 1871.

It is difficult to assess just how good *The Lamb* was because there is a confusion of evidence concerning the course over which he won his two Nationals.

The Druid in 'The Post and The Paddock' refers to 'the four miles and a quarter of the Liverpool Steeplechase', and whilst this was published in 1856 the supposedly first official survey of the course came in 1868 when it was measured at $4\frac{1}{2}$ miles and 30 yards. *The Lamb* as a six year old in 1868 won carrying 10st. 7lb. and the time was returned as 10 mins. 30 secs. His second win in 1871 at the age of nine was, according to the records, achieved in 9 mins. 36 secs. under 11st. 4lb. Yet a third source of information refers to the distance in 1868 as having been $4\frac{1}{4}$ miles.

These conflicting facts, therefore, make it impossible to place *The Lamb* in the same class as *Lottery*.

Disturbance (1873), *The Liberator* (1879), *Empress* (1880), the renowned *Frigate* who

---

* There were two horses of this name. The first *Peter Simple* was placed 3rd in 1841 and 1842 and second in 1845. The second *Peter Simple* was the winner in 1849 and 1853.

ran in seven Nationals (winning in 1889), and *Come Away* (1891) were all good winners which could really be regarded as outstanding even.

The year that *Come Away* won, 1891, was memorable, however, for an additional reason, for good horse that *Come Away* was, a better horse was second.

The 494 yards of the run-in deserve a volume to themselves or rather the events they have witnessed do. They have seen struggles for supremacy between tired horses and riders, they have seen weight finally take its measure of gallant horses; they have heard one rider, desperate to win the race, shout an offer of a substantial bribe to an opponent in an effort to achieve his ambition. In 1891 they saw a rider through sheer mulishness throw the race away.

Cloister 1893. Approaching the last, Harry Beasley on *Come Away* had a length or so to spare over Roddy Owen on *Cloister*. As they landed on the flat and started the long run-in Beasley had the inside position next to the rails yet Owen, who hated to go an inch further than necessary, persistently tried to come on Beasley's inside. The latter quite justifiably stuck to his ground and refused to let Owen come through. Owen's stubbornness was even more unforgivable when it is realized that *Cloister* was going the better of the two. When he finally did switch *Cloister* to the outside it was too late and *Come Away* won by half a length. It came to light after the race that *Come Away* had broken down at the last and Harry Beasley was nursing him home on three legs and admitted that if Owen had come outside him earlier *Cloister* would have won.

Owen vowed all kinds of things, amongst them that he would give Beasley the hiding of a lifetime. Richard Marsh, the trainer of *Cloister*, advised him not to try as he would probably come off second best again. Owen objected to the winner and whilst the case was aired before the Stewards a group of Irishmen almost lynched him there and then. The objection was overruled.

In 1892 *Cloister* was again second but the form was not good as he was giving 26lb. to a horse which was entitled to every ounce of it—*Father O'Flynn*—for he was a long way below *Cloister*'s class.

1893 was a different story altogether. *Cloister* was favourite and carried 12st. 7lb.

Once again he set off in front. He took hair-raising liberties with the fences but was very nimble footed and this quality proved his saviour more than once. After a circuit he was four lengths clear and as he passed the post he had forty lengths to spare over *Aesop*. The going had been firm and the time of 9 mins. $32\frac{2}{5}$ secs. was a new record. New records also were the winning margin and, of course, the weight carried.

He was entered again the following year and the handicapper allotted him 12st. 12lb. in his draft of the handicap, but when he copied it out to send to Messrs. Weatherby he wrote 12st. 7lb. by mistake. The public rushed to back him but the horse suffered several setbacks in his preparation and did not run. His first appearance that year was at Liverpool to win the Sefton with 13st. 3lb. by twenty lengths! This was the weight he was given in the National of 1895 but, once again, he was scratched a few days before the race.

Prior to this there had been some question of his entry for Liverpool not being accepted but this was solved satisfactorily. Apparently it had something to do with Mr. Duff's horses (of which *Cloister* was one) running in the name of 'Mr. Grant'.

Mystery prevailed again in 1896 but this time it concerned the whereabouts of the horse. Rumour had it that he was with Linde.

In fact he was being trained in great secrecy by Mr. Charles Thompson in the Whadden Chase country. On the two occasions when *Cloister* was scratched from the race the bookmakers seemed to hear of the event before anyone else, and he had accordingly gone out in the betting. Mr. Duff had been suspicious of the horse having been got at and at one stage had a bodyguard of plain clothes detectives guarding him in the Trainer's yard. Hence the secret preparations in 1896.

Shortly before the National Mr. Thompson incurred the displeasure of the Stewards and *Cloister's* future seemed uncertain.

For one reason or another he did not run at Aintree but won the Welsh Grand National two weeks after Aintree. A fortnight later he won the Great Shropshire Steeplechase after *Lady Grundrose* had been disqualified for carrying the wrong weight.

In eight seasons of racing he ran thirty-five times, winning nineteen of his races, being second in eight of them and third in another three.

National Heroes

One of the most interesting facts about *Cloister* was that he was bred by *Ascetic* who was a useless race-horse reduced to bringing the post from the village for Lord Fingall his owner, who had an equally useless mare *Grace II*. When the two were mated the result was *Cloister*, and *Ascetic* thereafter became one of the best sires of jumpers of his time. He sired two other Grand National winners in *Ascetic's Silver* (1906) and *Drumcree* (1903).

Manifesto 1897 and 1899. If one examines the racing histories of the one hundred and twenty-five National winners which there have been up to the present, none of them has an Aintree record which stands comparison to *Manifesto's* which reads:

1895   Aged 7, he finished 4th with 11st. 2lb. to *The Wild Man from Borneo*.

1896   Brought down at the first.

1897   Aged 9, he won by 20 lengths carrying 11st. 3lb.

1898   He met with an accident when he got loose from his box and in the course of jumping a 5 ft gate he rapped his fetlock and did not run for several months.

1899   Aged 11, he won easily by 5 lengths carrying 12st. 7lb. giving the second horse 25lb. and the third 35lb.

1900   He finished 3rd under the steadier of 12st. 13lb. giving the winner *Ambush II* 24lb. and *Barsac*, the second horse, every ounce of 38lb. He was eased near the finish as he obviously could not get to the winner, and *Barsac* got up on the post to be second.

1901   He did not run at all during this year.

1902   Aged 14, he finished 3rd carrying 12st. 8lb. giving the winner, 7 year old *Shannon Lass*, 35lb. and the second 38lb. (In this year also he ran second in The Grand Sefton 'Chase giving the winner *Kirkland* 35lb. *Kirkland* won the Grand National of 1905 with 11st. 5lb.)

1903   At the age of 15 he was 3rd once more but only carrying 12st. 3lb. this time—only 4 finished out of 23.

1904   At the age of 16 having been dropped in the weights to 12st. 1lb. he finished 9th to *Moifaa* who was exactly half his age, and to whom he was conceding 22lb. (His last appearance at Aintree was in the November of 1904 in The Valentine 'Chase when he finished the course, although unplaced, and was ridden by Frank Hartigan.)

Manifesto's achievements at Aintree are legendary and have never been equalled, let alone surpassed. Only *Cloister* and *Jerry M* even approach his standing as a National winner.

His first victory in 1897 at the age of nine was not a record breaking affair in itself but was so easily achieved as to be almost contemptuous.

Manifesto was bred by Mr. Harry Dyas in Co. Meath and it was in his name that he ran up to 1898. In the 1897 National Mr. Dyas had another entry—a mare called *Gentle Ida* of whom he had a great opinion and in fact preferred her to *Manifesto*. He put the pair on offer at £5,000 for the two and told Tom Vigors, the bloodstock agent, that he was convinced that one of them would win the National. *Gentle Ida* had won the Lancashire 'Chase in 1895 and had better public form than *Manifesto*. However, she was taken out of the race the day beforehand and *Manifesto*, trained by Willie McAuliffe, was a firm favourite at 6–1. There were 28 runners which included two previous winners in *The Wild Man from Borneo* and *The Soarer*, as well as other good horses such as *Cathal* and *Ford of Fyne*. From early on in the race *Timon* had made the running with *Manifesto* second. *The Soarer* came down at Valentine's on the second circuit and two out *Timon* blundered and dislodged his rider but was a tired horse when it happened. *Manifesto* was left in front, full of running, and the nearest rival as he jumped the last was a very remote *Cathal* who, in fact, fell at the last and *Manifesto* came home alone, 20 lengths clear of *Filbert*, with *Ford of Fyne* third.

Mr. Dyas sold *Manifesto* afterwards for a sum in the region of £4,000 to Mr. Bulteel. He also sold *Gentle Ida* for an even greater figure to Mr. Horatio Bottomley.

Manifesto's second victory in 1899 under 12st. 7lb. was in a time which was only four-fifths of a second slower than the 9 mins. 49 secs. in which he won his first National. The going at Aintree in 1899 was good although there had been some slight overnight frost. The field included *Sheriff Hutton*, the good French mare *Pistache*, *Manifesto's* former stable companion *Gentle Ida* who was favourite, and *Ambush II* running in the Prince of Wales' colours for the first time at Aintree.

Gentle Ida fell at Valentine's, *Pistache* fell at The Chair. At Valentine's on the second circuit *Barsac* led *Mum* and *Ambush*.

To protect the take-off and landing sides of the fences from the previous night's frost, hay or straw had been spread over the ground and that on the landing side of

80 *National Heroes*

60 Cloister (1893) with his owner Mr. C. G. Duff, who later became Sir Charles Asheton-Smith.

61 Manifesto (1897 and 1890).

62 Ambush II (1900) (A. Anthony up).

63 Jerry M. (1912) and Ernest Piggott.

64 Covercoat (1913).

65 Poethlyn (1919) and Ernest Piggott.

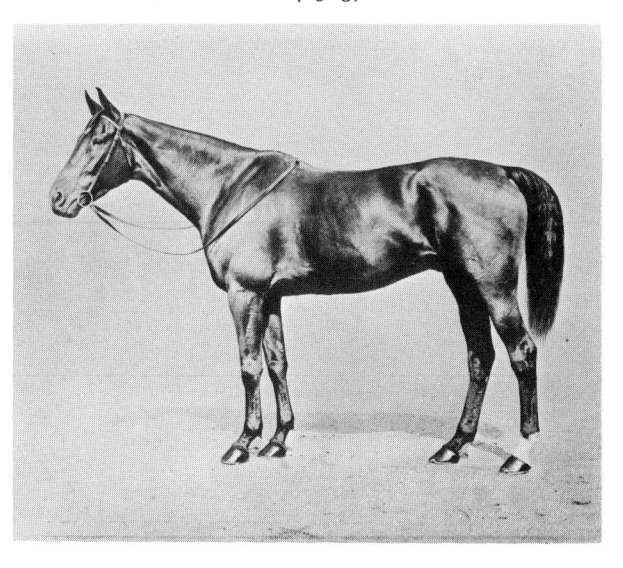

National Heroes 81

66 Troytown (1920) and Mr. J. Anthony.

67 Sergeant Murphy (1923) and Capt. G. Bennett.

68 Sprig (1927) with T. E. Leader.

69 Kellsboro' Jack (1933) and D. Williams.

70 Golden Miller (1934) with Gerry Wilson up.

71 Reynoldstown (1935 and 1936) with Mr. F. C. Furlong.

Valentine's had not been removed. *Manifesto* slipped on it, coming down on his shoulder. George Williamson, his jockey, said 'I saw one of his legs sticking straight up over my head in the air, the toe of my boot was on the ground and both irons were gone, but I left everything to *Manifesto* and he recovered himself. I picked up the reins and we went on'. From then on he began to improve steadily until by the time he jumped the last he was in front of everything and won comfortably by five lengths from *Ford of Fyne*.

1900. In 1900 *Manifesto* was carrying the top weight of 12st. 13lb. which was the burden the handicapper thought that he was capable of shouldering successfully, thus interpreting freely that the object of a handicap is to give every horse an equal chance of winning. *Manifesto* was asked to give as much as 48lb. to the bottom weights in the race.

Covert Hack fell at the first and *Barsac* and *Hidden Mystery* disputed the lead up to Becher's when *Barsac* went on. *Covert Hack* had found his feet and galloped on riderless with all the nuisance value of a loose horse finally putting *Hidden Mystery* out of the race at the very same fence at which he himself had fallen on the first circuit. After the second Valentine's *Ambush* went to the front and when he reached the last fence he was joined by *Manifesto* who had steadily made his way through the field under his burden of 12st. 13lb. As they came away from the last together a terrific struggle ensued. *Manifesto* was twelve years of age and *Ambush* six. In addition the younger horse had 25lb. advantage in the weights. Three hundred yards from the Post they were stride for stride. Two hundred yards out it was the same. The Stands were almost silent as they watched history being made but they were silent because they didn't know where their loyalties lay. They wanted so much a Royal victory but they also wanted *Manifesto*, their very own hero and idol, to be the first horse to win three Nationals. They didn't know which to cheer for or whether to cheer at all. A hundred yards out they still hadn't decided but finally *Ambush* came away in the last hundred yards to decide for them. A dead heat would have been the kindest result for neither horse deserved to lose but it was not to be and George Williamson eased *Manifesto* when he saw he had no chance of beating *Ambush*, and in the very last stride *Barsac* got up to take second place from *Manifesto*. And still the Stands didn't know whether to laugh or cry.

This achievement of *Manifesto* in 1900 was equal to his two victories in 1897 and 1899.

Even this was not the end of the *Manifesto* era and he figured in the placings again in 1902 and 1903.

Manifesto's breeding was as follows:

Manifesto b.g. 1888	Man O'War	Ben Battle	Rata Plan
			Young Alice
		Wisdom	Solon
			Conamara
	Vae Victis	King Victor	Fazzoletto
			Blue Bell
		The Ion Mare (un-named)	Ion
			Rhedycina

He was one of the best looking horses to win the National and his intelligence matched his looks.

Many people would consider themselves lucky to have owned one National winner but *Cloister's* owner, Mr. Charles Duff, was destined to own three. A short time after *Cloister* had won Mr. Duff became Sir Charles Assheton-Smith. From 1908 he had a number of horses in training with Bob Gore. Early in 1909 *Jerry M* was on offer at a reasonable sum and Gore was very keen to buy him.

Jerry M. *Jerry M* was bred in Ireland and called after the man who broke him and schooled him. As he was a very thick winded horse Sir Charles had a veterinary examination made and the report was not encouraging. However, Gore pressed him to buy the horse as he was convinced that there were some good races to be won with him before his breathing affected his ability. Even though he respected Gore's opinion Sir Charles had many misgivings before he finally parted with his cheque for £1,200.

In his first season for Gore he won the New Century Steeplechase at Hurst Park, the Stanley 'Chase at Liverpool, as well as The Becher, also at Liverpool, and a race at Kempton Park.

His first attempt at the National was as a seven-year-old in 1910 when he just failed by 3 lengths carrying 12st. 7lb. to give 30lb. to the winner, *Jenkinstown*. In the summer of that year he went to France to win the Paris Steeplechase at Auteuil.

Training difficulties were experienced the following year which prohibited him from going to Aintree for the freak race of 1911 when only the winner, *Glenside*, out of 33 starters, completed the course without either falling or being brought down in conditions like a glue-pot.

In 1912 his journey to Aintree was a strange one. There was a strike on at the time and his itinerary was as follows—From Worthing to London, where he spent the night in some stables near Victoria Station. The following morning he walked through Hyde Park to Marylebone Station on the second leg of his journey to Liverpool. However, his safe arrival was soon followed by the bookmakers installing him joint favourite at 4–1. Their estimate of him was shown to be correct when his sheet was taken off in the paddock. A season's absence from the racecourse had done him nothing but good but only one preparatory race before the National itself had caused the public to forsake him in the market. When they saw him stripped they soon changed their minds. Once again he was carrying 12st. 7lb. and was ridden by Ernest Piggott, an experienced Aintree rider. In the race he never put a foot wrong and gave his jockey an armchair ride winning by 6 lengths and 4 lengths from *Bloodstone* and *Axle Pin*.

Jerry M injured his pelvis muscles subsequent to his victory in the National (in which he became the third horse to carry 12st. 7lb. successfully), and did not run again that year. He was allotted 12st. 10lb. in the National of 1913 but did not run as he had finally gone completely in his wind. Gore and his owner won the race the following year with a horse called *Covercoat* who was a fairly good National winner carrying 11st. 6lb. but not as good as *Cloister* or *Jerry M*.

Jerry M's breeding was as follows:

Jerry M b.g. 1903	Walmsgate	Hampton	Lord Clifden
			Lady Langden
		Flying Footstep	Doncaster
			Atalanta
	The Luminary Mare (un-named)	Luminary	Beauclerk
			Stella
		Quinine	Sam Chifney
			Talipes

Troytown 1920. Quite obviously, different horses react in different ways to the Aintree fences and even in their post-1961 form they command respect. Their substance is very apparent and the very sight of them is sufficient to make an intelligent horse treat them with the caution they deserve, and if a horse is used to taking liberties with the fences on Park courses it is usually too late that he discovers that he cannot do the same with the Aintree fences.

Every so often there is a horse which has either the power of a bulldozer or the agility of a cat to help it survive brushes with the big Liverpool obstacles and *Troytown* had both. He was the boldest of jumpers and was a great strapping 17 hands with such a front and depth of girth that he looked small behind the saddle. Furthermore, his courage matched his size.

In the National of 1920 he was ridden by Jack Anthony who described him as more of a steam-engine than a horse for *Troytown* was always in a hurry—eager to get on with things. This characteristic was additional to having a very bad mouth and the combination of the two factors usually meant that the horse took charge of things and it was not until they met The Water jump, where he put in a superb leap but slipped on landing, that Anthony was able to get the upper hand. The horse took his time to recover but in spite of this he went off again still in the lead. His rider said he jumped clear into the air over Becher's and gave him the sensation similar to an express lift starting off. Four or five fences from home *Troytown* slipped on take-off and hit the fence so hard that Jack Anthony thought he had knocked it off the course. He galloped on as though nothing had happened. He stormed in an easy winner and his jockey managed to pull him up just before the first fence as he was starting a third circuit. He had won by twelve lengths from *The Turk II* and *The Bore* was a further six lengths behind in third place.

Troytown was bred by his owner, Major Thomas Collins-Gerrard and he was by *Zria* (by *Cyllene*) out of *Diane* by *Ascetic* out of *Forrest Queen*. He had run in the Stanley 'Chase at the National Meeting in 1919 but without success and was started again the following day for the Champion 'Chase which he won.

His career ended in tragedy. He had won the big French Steeplechase The Grand Prix at Auteuil in 1919 and contested it again in 1920 but did not have a clear run and finished third. He was started again on the Friday in the Prix des Drags. He broke his leg at one of the easiest obstacles on the course and had to be put down, and is buried not far from the course at Asnieres.

Poethlyn's win in 1919 under 12st. 7lb. and *Sprig* (1924) with 12st. 4lb. were both good weight carrying performances but neither returned an exceptionally fast time. *Sergeant Murphy's* time of 9 mins. 36 secs. under 11st. 3lb. was no mean performance for a horse aged thirteen, and considering he was barely 15·2 *Battleship's* win in 1938 carrying 11st. 6lb. was exceptionally good in a time of 9 mins. $29\frac{4}{5}$ secs. Indeed, between the Wars, i.e. from 1919 to 1940 inclusive, the weights carried and the times recorded by the National winners are in marked contrast to the years 1946–71. *Poethlyn*, *Troytown*, *Shaun Spadah*, *Music Hall*, *Sergeant Murphy*, *Sprigg*, *Gregalach*, *Shaun Goilin*, *Grakle*, *Kellsboro' Jack*, *Golden Miller*, *Reynoldstown* (twice), *Royal Mail* and *Battleship* all carried more than 11st., whereas since 1946 only *Freebooter*, *Early Mist*, *Royal Tan*, *E.S.B.*, *Sundew*, *Jay Trump* and *Gay Trip* have won with more than 11st.

After *Troytown* (1920) there is no winner of comparable stature until 1934, in which year *Golden Miller* won the race.

The Enigma of Golden Miller 1934. Probably the most accurate way to describe *Golden Miller* is as a brilliant 'chaser over Park courses, the winner of five Cheltenham Gold Cups, and also the winner of the 1934 Grand National.

Whilst one can say that he was probably one of the best horses to win the National it would not be correct to say that he was one of the best National winners. His first appearance at Aintree was in 1933 by which time he already had two Cheltenham Gold Cups to his credit and yet was then only six years old. The handicapper had imposed 12st. 2lb. He made a bad mistake at Becher's on the second circuit and although he recovered and jumped the next fence he fell at the Canal Turn.

The following year, with a third Gold Cup to his name, he came to Aintree again on the same handicap mark of 12st. 2lb. This time he got round and at the last fence *Delaneige* landed first just ahead of *Golden Miller*, *Forbra* and *Thomond II* but once on the flat *Golden Miller* sprinted away to win by five lengths. The time was a record 9 mins. $20\frac{2}{5}$ secs. which stands to this day.

In spite of his win *Golden Miller* could not be called an Aintree horse because he jumped off his forehand and the drop fences were made for horses which stand back at their fences.

In 1935, having added a fourth Gold Cup to his collection, *Golden Miller* was handicapped to carry 12st. 7lb. In fact this was only half the normal increase for a previous winner of the race to receive, but 12st. 7lb. was the maximum. *Golden Miller* only jumped nine fences before parting company with his rider at the tenth. He screwed on take-off and landed awkwardly. Of the relative few who actually witnessed the incident many were of the opinion that he had tried to refuse.

The following day he was started for The Champion 'Chase but made a mess of the first fence and once again deposited his rider on the floor. Only a short time before Aintree's National Meeting Cheltenham's race for the Gold Cup is run and in winning this in 1935 *Golden Miller* had had a very hard race indeed but his immediate victim in that contest was *Thomond II*. It has been suggested that neither horse had recovered from Cheltenham before they were started for the National but *Thomond* finished third in the National.

In 1936 *Golden Miller*, now with a fifth Cheltenham Gold Cup to his credit, was again started for the National but fell at the first fence. In 1937 he refused at the twelfth.

Somewhat ironically *Golden Miller's* win in 1934 has, because of its record time, been the yardstick by which all National winners have been rated ever since.

88 National Heroes

72 Battleship (1938) with Bruce Hobbs.

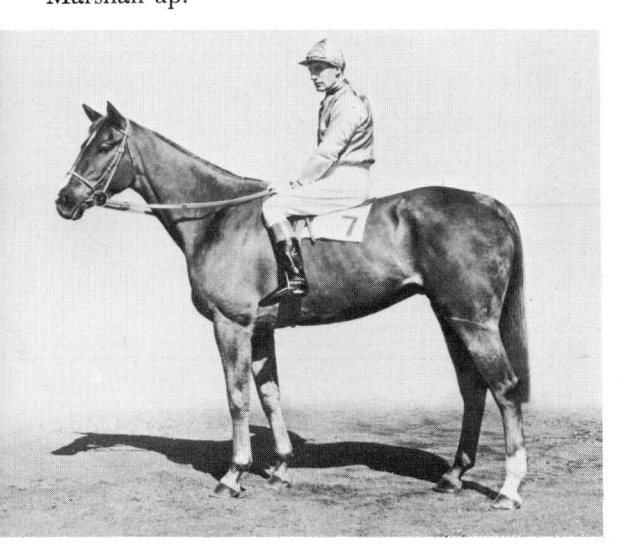

73. Freebooter (1950) and J. Power.

74 Teal (1952) and A. P. Thompson.

75 **Early Mist** (1953) with Bryan Marshall up.

76 Royal Tan (1954).

77 Quare Times (1955) and Pat Taaffe.

National Heroes 89

78 E.S.B. (1956) with D. V. Dick.

79 Sundew (1957) and F. T. Winter.

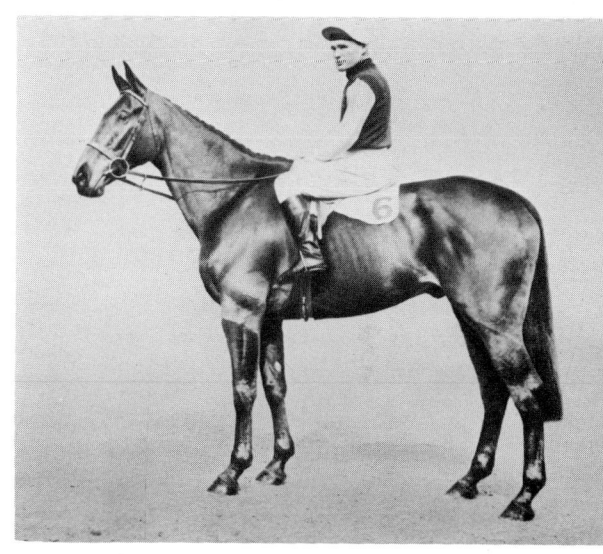

80 Oxo (1959). M. Scudamore up.

81 Merryman II (1960).

82 Jay Trump (1965) and Mr. T. Smith.

This persistence on the part of Miss Paget, who owned *Golden Miller*, in sending him to Aintree repeatedly is a reflection of the pre-War status of the Grand National as compared to the Gold Cup. The Miller's five Gold Cup victories netted a total of £3,350 for his owner—but this was still less than half of the £7,265 which his single National victory brought.

And so this horse, so brilliant over Park courses, must be classified as the most enigmatic of National winners. Thirty years later and in another ownership he would not have seen Aintree.

Reynoldstown 1935/6. *Reynoldstown*, the most recent of the dual-National winners, came within three fifths of a second of equalling *Golden Miller's* record time. Although an exceptionally fine 'chaser the circumstances of his second National success preclude him from ranking with such names as *Manifesto* and *Cloister*.

1950 Freebooter. The 1950 success of *Freebooter* carrying 11st. 11lb. in 9 mins. $23\frac{2}{5}$ secs. must rank as the outstanding performance in the post-War Grand Nationals. His winning margin of fifteen lengths with ten lengths between the second and third in a field of forty-nine speaks for itself, and doubtless had there been more opposition in the closing stages he would have returned an even faster time. His victories at Aintree both before and after his National success stamp him as a true Aintree horse, for besides the National he won The Champion 'Chase, the Grand Sefton (with 12st. 7lb.) and The Becher, all at Aintree, as well as sixteen other races elsewhere.

By *Steel Point* he was a thick-set bay with a powerful front and shoulders. His Aintree victories prior to the National of 1950 fully entitled him to the 11st. 11lb. which the handicapper allotted him and he started joint favourite with Lord Bicester's *Roimond*. In the field also were Lord Mildmay's *Cromwell* ridden by his owner, the winner of the previous year, *Russian Hero*, *Cloncarrig* and *Monaveen*.

The first fence claimed *Zarter*, *Cottage Welcome*, *Skouras* and *Russian Hero* amongst others. The sorry tale continued and almost included *Freebooter* at the Chair fence where he stood back too far and almost demolished it. Somehow Jimmy Power stayed aboard and from then onwards *Freebooter* never put a foot wrong. *Cloncarrig* led from the second Valentine's up to the 29th fence where his concentration wavered at the sound of *Freebooter's* galloping as he ranged alongside him. They took off together but *Freebooter's* presence had caused *Cloncarrig* to misjudge it and down he came. There was nothing to challenge *Freebooter* and he jumped the last well and galloped home a very easy winner.

In 1951 he was a victim of the bad start and was brought down at the second fence. The following year carrying 12st. 7lb. again as he had done in 1951, he fell at the Canal Turn on the second circuit when going well in the lead, with *Teal* the ultimate winner.

The post-National years of the many heroes which the race has produced have been spent in a variety of ways. *Lottery* ended up as the lead horse in a stage-coach.

When *Voluptuary's* racing days were over he was bought by the actor Leonard Boyle and appropriately they played at Drury Lane in the Grand National scene from 'The Prodigal Daughter'. They had to jump a water jump and Boyle's part consisted of falling into the water for which he received an extra 5/–.

The Colonel, *Austerlitz*, *Disturbance* and *Reugny* took up Stud duties but none of them got anything great.

Empress, however, *was* a success at Stud and when mated with *Kendal* produced *Red Prince II* who was a good horse on the flat as a two-year-old and later won several Steeplechases before becoming a successful sire of jumpers.

Some National winners never won a race again—*Tipperary Tim* and *Mr. What* to name but two. There are many knowledgeable racing authorities who claim that a horse is never the same after the National. But what of horses like *Eremon* who won the National and then carried a 12lb. penalty to win the Lancashire 'Chase shortly afterwards, and won two races besides—all four races within the space of twenty-four days!

Ilex was another who won the Lancashire 'Chase shortly after the National. *Salamander* won the Grand Annual Steeplechase at Warwick only seven days after his National win, and *Gamecock* certainly lived up to his name when he won The

Champion 'Chase at Aintree the very next day after winning the National. He went on running and winning for a further eight years—until he was sixteen, in fact.

And on this topic one cannot forget that hero of all heroes—*Manifesto*—who, at the age of sixteen carried 12st. 1lb. in the National and got round, for the seventh time.

Not all National heroes have won the race and in the unsaddling enclosure for the second horse at Liverpool there are two plaques—one to the memory of *Macmoffat* and the other to another gallant Scottish horse—*Wyndburgh*. *Macmoffat* was second in consecutive years (1939 and 1940), whilst *Wyndburgh* was second in 1957, 1959 and 1962. Another Scottish horse, *Freddie*, was second in successive years also. Like these three have been many who were consistently placed in the National without ever achieving victory. *Seventy-Four* and the first *Peter Simple* head this list which includes *The Knight of Gwynne, Sir John, Weathercock, Xanthus, Arbury*, and more recently *Tiberretta, Tudor Line, Irish Lizard* and many others in the years between.

Heroes, also, were riders like Tim Brookshaw who rode *Wyndburgh* to be second after breaking an iron at the second Becher's, and men like Mr. Harry Brown who having dislocated a shoulder remounted *The Bore* to jump the last fence and finish second. Charles Boyce's feat in riding with his arm strapped to his side to win on *Emigrant* was another heroic performance. The late Sir Jack Jarvis in his autobiography wrote:

Newey's feat in riding *Eremon* to victory in the 1907 Grand National after breaking a stirrup leather at the second fence was one of the finest and pluckiest bits of riding I have ever seen. When Newey came into the weighing room after the race, the inside of his thighs were bleeding where they had been badly chafed.

For every one of these instances of human and equine achievement there must be a score of others which have not been recorded, but the ones which have been are enough to show the kind of challenge which Aintree and The National have to offer.

7.
The Changing Shape of The National

Inevitably the Grand National has always been regarded with mixed feelings and although a favourable attitude has prevailed for most of the time there have been periods when the criticisms out-numbered the praises.

The injuries caused to both horses and riders by the Stone Wall fence in the early years brought much justified protest. Again in the period between 1850 and 1860 there were charges of malpractice concerning the handicap and the discrepancies in form shown by many horses. The shortening in price of a horse which caused the public to rush to back it before the odds contracted further and then its withdrawal was another of the sharp practices which prompted the observation that 'many things were done in that green leaf which are not now done in the dry'.

The outcry following the incident at the Canal Turn in 1928 which put twenty or more horses out of the race resulted in a Bill in Parliament to ban the sport.

The disaster at the first fence in 1951, the tragedy of *Devon Loch* in 1956, and the pile-up at the twenty-third fence in 1967 were other occasions when feelings ran high and brought accusations of cruelty against the promoters of the race and the owners and trainers who entered their horses.

What amounts to cruelty will vary according to one's outlook and ethics, but it is probably universally acceptable to say that once it is realized that certain circumstances cause pain, suffering or distress in one form or another then the bringing about or causing the continuance of those circumstances would be definite acts of cruelty. The honest belief that a horse can jump the fences and will stay the distance and entering him in the race can never amount to an act of cruelty. Forcing the horse to continue once it is apparent that his abilities have been taxed to the limit may well amount to cruelty on the part of the rider, but I cannot recall an incident of this kind in the National, and invariably the horse itself will indicate its condition by a refusal.

A number of accidents at a particular fence must give cause for concern, and although there has been only one case in recent years where the Water jump caused a serious injury, a number of people regard it as potentially dangerous.

Physical overcrowding in the early stages of the race has caused many fallers in the past—often enough to make the continued practice of permitting such large

83 The loose horse is first past the post but Battleship (left) beats Royal Danieli by a short head. There has never been a dead-heat for the National nor any photograph finish equipment to record such an event but several times in the history of the race two horses have crossed the line virtually as one.

84 1968 Red Alligator wins by twenty lengths.

85 Oxo (M. Scudamore) beats Wyndburgh whose rider, Tim Brookshaw, had been without irons since the second Becher's.

numbers to run in the race debatable as to whether it amounts to cruelty or not.

However, it is well to remember that the course has had a century and a quarter in which to reveal its faults and dangers and some incidents which arise are isolated and are unlikely to be repeated.

Yet, underlying these circumstances which provoked so much criticism in 1928, 1951, 1956 and 1967 was the formula which made the National so popular, namely a large number of horses running over a very testing course which resulted in three of every four being put out of the race. It catered for a public which was present at various points of the big two and a quarter mile circuit at Aintree. For those spectators watching the race at points such as the Canal Turn or Anchor Bridge the numerical size of the field was everything for all the thrills had to be packed into those few seconds during which the runners were clearly visible to them. Obviously the noise created by forty, fifty or sixty horses as they galloped and as they brushed through

The Changing Shape of The National

the tops of the fences gave atmosphere and created tension and with so many horses reaching a jump in quick succession it was a reasonable supposition that some incident would take place at almost every fence.

This simple formula proved a crowd-puller from the very first for as the correspondent of the Liverpool Courier wrote after the 1839 race—'All men of ardent feelings love moderate danger for the very excitement which it produces, and the intrepidity which it brings into action'.

The attendance figure for that year was estimated at between forty and fifty thousand. In the late 1930s and again after the war up to 1960 as many as 300,000 went to Aintree each year to watch the race. The revenue from such attendances enabled the Aintree executive to make the race so valuable.

86 Team Spirit beats Purple Silk.

Televising the race had several consequences—firstly, whilst it reduced the Aintree attendance figures to a fraction of what they had been, it boosted those at other courses. Secondly, it made the whole race visible to an estimated viewing audience of something like 10,000,000 in the British Isles alone.

The fees from Television compensated for the loss of revenue from the decreased attendances and from 1961 to 1964 the race was sponsored firstly by Messrs. Schweppes and then by the Irish Hospitals Sweepstakes. Currently the Levy Board contribute £10,000 to the added money.

The increased popularity of National Hunt Racing shown by the attendance figures at almost every other racecourse under the Jockey Club jurisdiction is directly attributable to the televised Grand National and the race has become an annual showpiece for the sport.

As the B.B.C. bases its estimate of a programme on viewing figures and because the Levy Board realize its value to the sport generally it is true to say that the Grand National still exists on the strength of public opinion.

Making the complete race visible to many people virtually for the first time resulted in a new kind of race-viewer who is simultaneously more appreciative yet more critical. His first taste of Steeplechasing at Aintree was in 1960 when *Merryman II* won. The first two days of the Meeting had produced three fatal accidents and in the National itself there was a fourth, and if it is exciting to 'danger freely court' for most people the experience of its proximity is as much as they want and when it materializes in the form of tragedy they turn away. Thus the National did not have the best of television debuts.

As the success of the National had been at virtually two levels—with the public as a spectacle, and with owners because of its value—so now the threat of dissatisfaction with the form of the race was at two levels also.

The danger of losing popularity with the public meant decreased attendance figures which in turn meant loss of revenue for National Hunt racing. Loss of sympathy amongst owners meant the absence of the best horses. It was in an attempt to change the image of the National that the two measures of confining the top weight in the handicap to 12st. and the sloping of the take-off sides to the fences were taken.

87 Ayala comes again to beat Carrickbeg.

88 1961. Nicolaus Silver wins from the 1960 winner Merryman II with O'Malley Point, Scottish Flight II and Kilmore, the winner of 1962, in close attendance. Team Spirit who was to win in 1964 finished 9th, Mr. What the winner of 1958 was 10th. Oxo who won in 1959 had also been in the field.

At the time these steps were regarded by many people as being revolutionary but even with such improvements the last ten Nationals have not given any good reasons for complacency. Of 388 horses which started for the race between 1961–70 some 70 per cent were still in the race after a circuit, but only 40 per cent finished the course. Fifty-nine per cent of the runners either falling, being brought down or departing from the race in one way or another, and a further 1 per cent being put out by accidents which were fatal are figures which are hardly likely to further the cause of Steeplechasing in a community which has been described as a nation of animal lovers.

The second level at which the National's popularity began to wane was amongst the ranks of owners and trainers. With the advent of Sponsored races they had alternatives to the National and Aintree was no longer the summit of the National Hunt year.

Whereas *Golden Miller's* five Cheltenham Gold Cups in the 1930s brought Miss Paget, his owner, less than half the amount he earned by his one Grand National victory, *Arkle* in the 1960s never ran at Aintree yet won his owner almost four times the amount of prize-money which victory in the richest ever National would have brought.

From being virtually the only race of any real value for good staying steeplechasers the National has become the one valuable race which these horses miss in such numbers that in the 1970 National only one horse carried more than 11st. and that was the 11st. 5lb. carried by the winner. A further ten carried weights between 10st. 13lb. and 10st. 1lb. and the remaining seventeen were all weighted at 10st.

Nor was it a case of many of the top weights being taken out of the race; of sixty-eight entries only six were given more than 11st. and the other sixty-two were handicapped between 10st. and 10st. 13lb.

Only seven finished from twenty-eight Starters. The quality of the field, or lack of it, was further reflected in the time returned by the winner which was 9 mins. 38 secs. In view of the ideal conditions this was far from good.

At first glance it seemed that the 19lb. which the winner was conceding to each of the other six finishers was far from sufficient especially as the second horse was twenty lengths away. Of course the need was not for an extension of the handicap but a division of the race.

Without the winner it would have been a good finish, but either with or without him it was not what one would expect from a promotion which claims to be the Blue Riband of Steeplechasing.

The old recipe for attracting the best horses to Aintree, namely the sheer weight of prize-money, is no longer available. In 1946 the National was worth £8,805 as against the Cheltenham Gold Cup's £1,130. In 1970 the Cheltenham Gold Cup was worth £8,103 to the winner; The Whitbread Gold Cup £7,136; the Hennessey Gold Cup £6,090; The Benson & Hedges Gold Cup £5,119; The Scottish Grand National £5,533. To put the Grand National on a plane as financially superior as the one it enjoyed twenty-five years ago would take a sum in excess of £60,000.

Even then it would not be certain to attract the best horses for it is doubtful whether *Arkle* would have been subjected to the risks involved in running in the National whatever the value of the race had been.

Furthermore, *Arkle's* owner is not alone in this outlook.

Yet it is not the course as much as the type of race which deters these owners from entering their horses for Steeplechasing's richest prize. Fears of interference from loose horses and all the risks attendant on the big fields which usually start for the National are uppermost in their minds.

The statement of the problem thirty-five years ago by The Hon. Geo. Lambton holds good today. The Grand National is a race for good horses and that entails excluding anything less than the best. How ineffective the present Conditions of Entry are in this respect was all too apparent when recently a horse qualified for the National by virtue of a walk-over. *Permit*, the horse in question, is undoubtedly a worthy candidate for the National and subsequently won a race which would have qualified him anyway, but the same circumstances involving another horse might have a totally different outcome.

The changes made to the wording of the Conditions of Entry for 1970 merely took into account the general increase in prize-money which has taken place in racing generally during the last few years so that the relevant section reads:

For horses which at closing and since November 1, 1967 have won or been placed second, third or fourth over the Grand National course, or have won a Steeplechase of three miles or upwards to the advertised value of £650 or with at least £550 added to Stakes; or have won a Steeplechase of any distance value £750.

It will be recalled that in the 1969 Conditions of Entry the corresponding figures were £500, £400 and £600.

It is difficult to see how in the last mentioned case, i.e. a winner of a Steeplechase of, for example, 2 miles, is a suitable candidate for Aintree merely because the race was worth £750.

There is a lot to be said in favour of making certain races qualifying races. The Eider 'Chase at Newcastle comes to mind as one and obviously winning or being placed in races over part of the National course should also carry the necessary qualifications.

A field made up of invited entries has great appeal and also the advantages which an unprejudiced selection would automatically carry with it. The invitations could be extended from a panel of (three) Jockey Club handicappers. Such a system would give the race more prestige than it has ever had and this could well succeed where prize-money would fail.

How far the Cheltenham Gold Cup and Grand National affect each other by being so close together in the Calendar is another point which would not suffer from investigation. Likewise a rider's qualifications to ride in the race.

The injustices wrought by the handicap in past Grand Nationals must make its retention in its present form a subject for very careful consideration. Who would have begrudged *Manifesto* a third National, or *Merryman II* another victory in 1961, or *Prince Regent* even his first? And these are only three cases amongst many.

The purpose of a handicap is to bring as many horses as possible together at the end of the race, but the number of times that more than two horses have been concerned in the finish of the National could be counted on the fingers of one hand. And this must be the yardstick which measures the effectiveness of the handicap system.

89 The best finish for many years. Bryan Marshall gets Royal Tan home by a neck from Tudor Line (G. Slack).

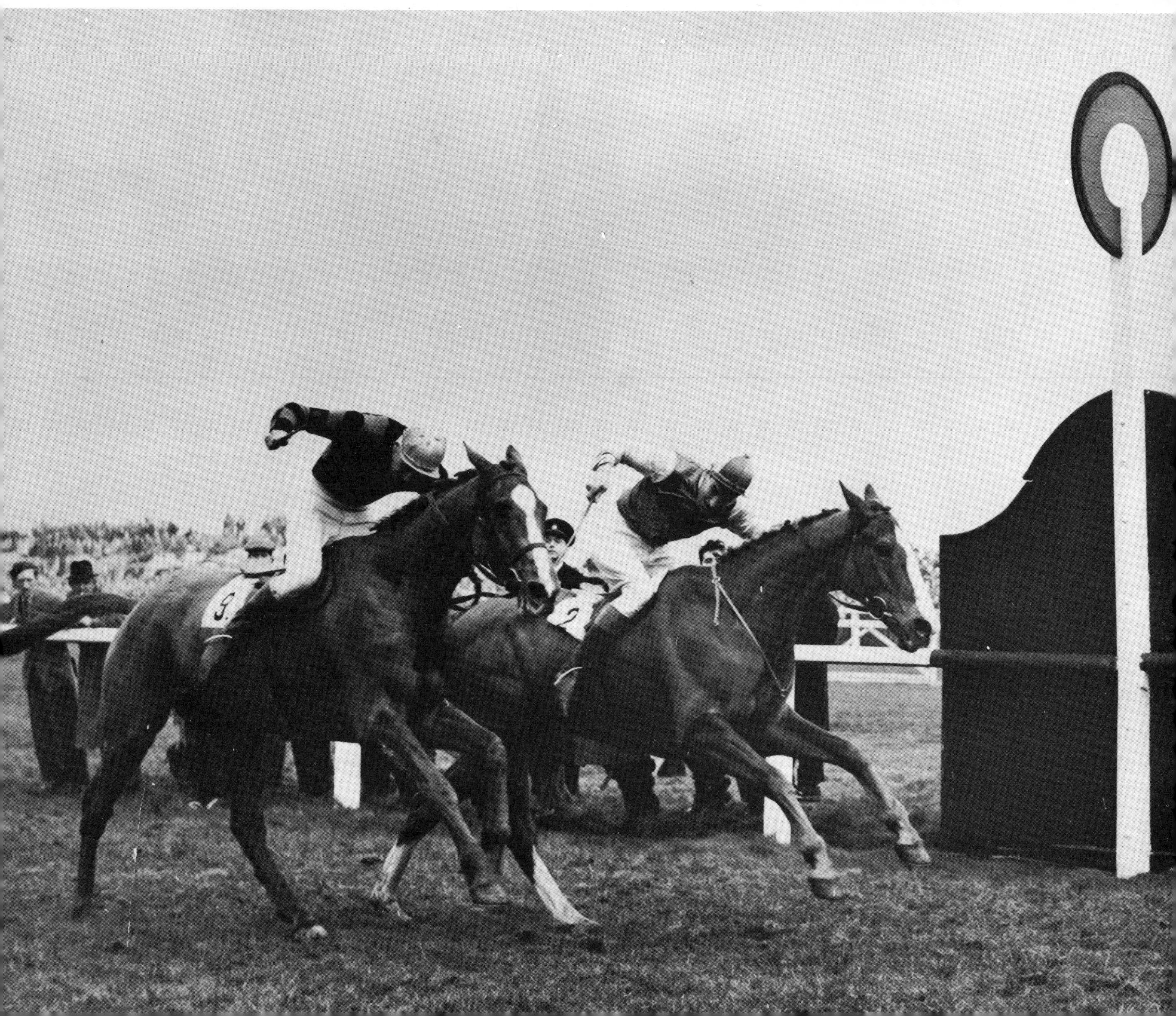
9
2

Large fields and handicaps are virtually synonymous but it is doubtful whether a field in excess of twenty-five benefits the race in any way and limiting the race to the top twenty-five horses in a handicap with a range of 18lb. or 21lb. (12st.–10st. 10lb. or 10st. 7lb.) would probably produce far better races and much closer finishes. Certainly such conditions are more likely to attract the best horses than those which prevail at present, and on the basis that the National in its Televised form is the one that commands consideration, then the need for great numbers of horses is no longer a factor. One horse in the Foxhunter's 'Chase at Aintree in 1970 brought as much drama to the Television screen as twenty-eight did in the National.

Finally, whatever changes are made in the future they must ensure an equitable result in that the biggest prize in Steeplechasing goes to the best horse.

90 Left to right—Sandy Sprite (R. Barry) 5th., Black Secret (Mr. J. Dreaper) 2nd., Bowgeeno (G. Thorner) 4th., and the winner Specify (J. Cook) who jumped the last in fifth place. Astbury (J. Bourke) is out of the picture to the left.

8.
The Winners and Placed Horses, 1837—1970.

Year	Result 1st. 2nd. 3rd.	Age & Weight	Rider	Trainer	Runners	S.P.	Time M.Secs.	Going
1837	**The Duke** The Disowned only 2 finished	—	Mr. H. Potts	—	6	—	—	
1838	**Sir Henry** Scamp The Duke	—	T. Olliver	—	10	—	—	
1839	**Lottery** Seventy-four Paulina	a–12–0 a–12–0 a–12–0	J. Mason T. Olliver Mr. Martin	Dockeray	17	5–1	14.53	f
1840	**Jerry** Arthur Valentine	a–12–0 a–12–0 a–12–0	B. Bretherton Mr. A. McDonough Mr. Power	—	13	12–1 8–1 —	12.30	g
1841	**Charity** Cigar Peter Simple	a–12–0 a–12–0 a–12–0	Mr. Powell Mr. A. McDonough Walker	—	10	14–1 4–1 6–1	13.25	g
1842	**Gay Lad** Seventy-four Peter Simple	a–12–0 a–12–0 a–12–0	T. Olliver Powell Mr. Hunter	—	15	7–1 6–1 6–1	13.30	g

The Winners and Placed Horses, 1837–1970

Year	Result 1st. 2nd. 3rd.	Age & Weight	Rider	Trainer	Runners	S.P.	Time M.Secs.	Going
1843	**Vanguard**	a–11–10	T. Olliver	—	16	12–1	—	g/f
	Nimrod	a–11–0	Scott			10–1		
	Dragsman	a–11–3	Crickmere			10–1		
1844	**Discount**	a–10–12	Crickmere	—	15	5–1	—	s
	The Returned	a–12–0	Scott			15–1		
	Tom Tug	a–10–7	Rackley			—		
1845	**Cureall**	a–11–5	Loft	—	15	—	10.47	s
	Peter Simple	a–11–12	Frisby			9–1		
	The Exquisite	a–11–12	Byrne			—		
1846	**Pioneer**	6–11–12	Taylor	—	22	—	10.46	g
	Culverthorpe	a–11–4	Rackley			12–1		
	Switcher	5–12–4	Wynne			—		
1847	**Mathew**	a–10–6	D. Wynne	—	26	10–1	10.39	g
	St. Leger	a–12–3	T. Olliver			15–1		
	Jerry	a–11–6	Bradley			100–8		
1848	**Chandler**	a–11–12	Capt. Little	—	29	12–1	11.21	s
	The Curate	a–11–12	T. Olliver			6–1		
	The British Yeoman	a–11–4	Mr. Bevill			—		
1849	**Peter Simple**	a–11–0	T. Cunningham	—	24	20–1	10.56	s
	The Knight of Gwynne	a–10–7	Capt. D'Arcy			8–1		
	Prince George	a–10–10	T. Olliver			5–1		
1850	**Abd-el-Kader**	a–9–12	C. Green	—	32	—	9.57½	g
	The Knight of Gwynne	a–11–8	Wynne			12–1		
	Sir John	a–11–8	J. Ryan			7–1		
1851	**Abd-el-Kader**	a–10–4	T. Abbott	—	21	7–1	9.59	g/s
	Maria Day	a–10–5	J. Frisby			100–6		
	Sir John	a–11–12	J. Ryan			7–1		

The Winners and Placed Horses, 1837–1970 107

Year	Result 1st. 2nd. 3rd.	Age & Weight	Rider	Trainer	Runners	S.P.	Time M.Secs.	Going
1852	**Miss Mowbray**	a–10–4	Mr. A. Goodman	Dockeray	24	—	9.58½	g
	Maurice Daley	a–9–4	C. Boyce			—		
	Sir Peter Laurie	a–11–2	W. Holman			30–1		
1853	**Peter Simple**	a–10–10	T. Olliver	—	21	9–1	10.37½	s
	Miss Mowbray	a–10–12	Mr. Gordon			5–1		
	Oscar	a–10–2	Mr. A. Goodman			6–1		
1854	**Bourton**	a–11–12	Tasker	—	20	4–1f	9.59	g
	Spring	6–9–10	W. Archer			20–1		
	Crabbs	a–9–2	D. Wynne			10–1		
1855	**Wanderer**	a–9–8	J. Hanlon	—	20	25–1	10.25	s
	Free Trader	6–9–4	Meaney			50–1		
	Maurice Daley	a–9–6	R. James			20–1		
1856	**Free Trader**	a–9–6	G. Stevens	—	21	25–1	10.9½	g
	Minerva	6–9–10	Sly, Junr.			25–1		
	Minos	a–9–4	R. James			50–1		
1857	**Emigrant**	a–9–10	C. Boyce	—	28	10–1	10.6	h
	Weathercock	6–8–12	Green			25–1		
	Treachery	5–9–0	Poole			50–1		
1858	**Little Charlie**	a–10–7	W. Archer	—	16	100–6	11.5	h
	Weathercock	7–11–7	Mr. Edwards			25–1		
	Xanthus	a–11–0	F. Balchin			33–1		
1859	**Half Caste**	6–9–7	C. Green	—	20	7–1	10.2	g
	Jean du Quesne	a–9–9	H. Lamplugh			10–1		
	The Huntsman	6–11–2	B. Land, Junr.			100–8		
1860	**Anatis**	a–9–10	Mr. Thomas	—	19	7–2f	—	g
	The Huntsman	7–11–8	Capt. Townley			33–1		
	Xanthus	a–10–0	F. Balchin			10–1		

The Winners and Placed Horses, 1837–1970

Year	Result 1st. 2nd. 3rd.	Age & Weight	Rider	Trainer	Runners	S.P.	Time M.Secs.	Going
1861	**Jealousy**	a–9–12	J. Kendall	—	24	5–1	10.14	g
	The Dane	5–10–0	W. White			33–1		
	Old Ben Roe	a–10–7	G. Waddington			10–1		
1862	**The Huntsman**	a–11–0	H. Lamplugh	—	13	3–1f	9.30	g
	Bridegroom	a–10–13	B. Land. Junr.			10–1		
	Romeo	a–8–12	Mr. C. Bennett			100–8		
1863	**Emblem**	a–10–10	G. Stevens	—	16	4–1	11.20	g
	Arbury	a–11–2	Mr. Goodman			25–1		
	Yaller Gal	a–10–13	Mr. Dixon			20–1		
1864	**Emblematic**	6–10–6	G. Stevens	—	25	10–1	11.50	g
	Arbury	a–11–12	B. Land, Junr.			40–1		
	Chester	a–10–0	W. White			40–1		
1865	**Alcibiade**	5–11–4	Capt. Coventry	—	23	100–7	11.16	h
	Hall Court	6–11–0	Capt. Tempest			50–1		
	Emblematic	7–11–10	G. Stevens			5–1		
1866	**Salamander**	a–10–7	Mr. A. Goodman	—	30	40–1	9.58½	h
	Cortolvin	a–11–6	J. Page			8–1		
	Creole	a–10–10	G. Waddington			15–1		
1867	**Cortolvin**	a–11–13	J. Page	—	23	100–6	10.42	g
	Fan	5–10–3	Thorpe			8–1		
	Shangarry	9–10–13	Mr. Thomas			100–7		
1868	**The Lamb**	6–10–7	Mr. Edwards	Ben Land	21	10–1	10.30	h
	Pearl Diver	a–10–12	Tomlinson			9–1		
	Alcibiade	8–11–10	Col. Knox			100–6		
1869	**The Colonel**	6–10–7	G. Stevens	—	22	13–1	11.0	g
	Hall Court	10–10–12	Capt. Tempest			66–1		
	Gardener	a–10–7	Ryan			66–1		

Year	Result 1st. 2nd. 3rd.	Age & Weight	Rider	Trainer	Runners	S.P.	Time M.Secs.	Going
1870	**The Colonel**	7–11–12	G. Stevens	—	23	4–1f	10.9½	g
	The Doctor	a–11–7	G. Holman			5–1		
	Primrose	6–10–12	Mr. W. R. Brockton			10–1		
1871	**The Lamb**	9–11–4	Mr. Thomas	—	25	5–1	9.36	g
	Despatch	a–10–0	G. Waddington			10–1		
	Scarrington	a–11–4	Cranshaw			60–1		
1872	**Casse Tete**	a–10–0	J. Page	—	25	20–1	10.14½	f
	Scarrington	a–11–2	R. I'Anson			100–1		
	Despatch	a–10–4	G. Waddington			4–1		
1873	**Disturbance**	6–11–11	Mr. J. Richardson	J. Richardson	28	20–1	—	g
	Rhysworth	a–11–8	Boxall			8–1		
	Columbine	a–10–9	Harding			50–1		
1874	**Reugny**	6–10–12	Mr. J. Richardson	J. Richardson	22	5–1f	10.4	g
	Chimney Sweep	a–10–2	J. Jones			—		
	Merlin	a–10–7	J. Adams			40–1		
1875	**Pathfinder**	a–10–11	Mr. Thomas	—	19	100–6	10.22	h
	Dainty	a–11–0	Mr. Hathaway			25–1		
	La Venie	5–11–12	J. Page			6–1		
1876	**Regal**	5–11–3	J. Cannon	J. Cannon	19	25–1	11.14	g
	Congress	a–11–3	Mr. E. P. Wilson			25–1		
	Shifnal	a–10–3	R. I'Anson			100–3		
1877	**Austerlitz**	5–10–8	Mr. F. Hobson	—	16	15–1	10.10	g
	Congress	a–12–7	J. Cannon			20–1		
	The Liberator	a–10–12	Mr. Thomas			25–1		
1878	**Shifnal**	a–10–12	J. Jones	—	12	100–15	10.23	g
	Martha	a–10–9	Mr. T. Beasley			20–1		
	Pride of Kildare	a–11–7	Mr. J. Moore			6–1		

The Winners and Placed Horses, 1837-1970

Year	Result 1st. 2nd. 3rd.	Age & Weight	Rider	Trainer	Runners	S.P.	Time M.Secs.	Going
1879	**The Liberator**	a–11–4	Mr. G. Moore	Moore	18	5–1	10.12	g
	Jackal	a–11–0	J. Jones			1000–65		
	Martha	a–10–13	Mr. T. Beasley			50–1		
1880	**Empress**	5–10–7	Mr. T. Beasley	H. Linde	14	8–1	10.20	g
	The Liberator	a–12–7	Mr. G. Moore			11–2		
	Downpatrick	6–10–7	Gavin			100–15		
1881	**Woodbrook**	7–11–3	Mr. T. Beasley	H. Linde	13	6–1f	11.50	h
	Regal	10–11–12	Jewitt			11–1		
	Thornfield	5–10–9	R. Marsh			11–2		
1882	**Seaman**	6–11–6	Lord Manners	Jewitt	12	10–1	10.42$\frac{3}{5}$	h
	Cyrus	5–10–9	Mr. T. Beasley			9–2		
	Zoedone	5–10–0	Capt. Smith			20–1		
1883	**Zoedone**	6–11–0	Count C. Kinsky	W. H. P. Jenkins	10	100–8	11.39	h
	Black Prince	a–10–4	Canavan			100–3		
	Downpatrick	9–10–7	Mr. T. Widger			100–7		
1884	**Voluptuary**	6–10–5	Mr. E. Wilson	T. Wilson	15	10–1	10.5	h
	Frigate	6–11–3	Mr. H. Beasley			10–1		
	Roquefort	5–10–5	J. Childs			9–1		
1885	**Roquefort**	6–11–0	Mr. E. Wilson	Swatton	19	100–30f	10.10	g
	Frigate	7–11–10	Mr. H. Beasley			7–1		
	Black Prince	a–10–5	T. Skelton			33–1		
1886	**Old Joe**	7–10–9	T. Skelton	Douglas	23	25–1	10.14$\frac{3}{5}$	g
	Too Good	a–11–12	Mr. H. Beasley			7–1		
	Gamecock	7–10–12	W. E. Stephens			50–1		
1887	**Gamecock**	8–11–0	W. Daniells	Jordan	16	20–1	10.10$\frac{1}{5}$	g
	Savoyard	a–10–13	T. Skelton			100–14		
	Johnny Longtail	a–10–6	J. Childs			40–1		

The Winners and Placed Horses, 1837–1970 111

Year	Result 1st. 2nd. 3rd.	Age & Weight	Rider	Trainer	Runners	S.P.	Time M.Secs.	Going
1888	**Playfair**	7–10–7	Mawson	T. Cannon	20	40–1	10.12	g
	Frigate	10–11–2	Mr. W. Beasley			100–8		
	Ballot Box	a–12–4	W. Nightingall			25–1		
1889	**Frigate**	11–11–4	Mr. T. Beasley	—	20	8–1	10.1⅕	g
	Why Not	8–11–5	Mr. C. J. Cunningham			100–9		
	M.P.	a–10–9	A. Nightingall			20–1		
1890	**Ilex**	6–10–5	A. Nightingall	Nightingall	16	4–1f	10.41⅘	g
	Pau	a–10–3	Halsey			100–1		
	M.P.	a–11–5	Mr. W. H. Moore			8–1		
1891	**Come Away**	7–11–12	Mr. H. Beasley	H. Beasley	21	4–1f	9.58	g
	Cloister	7–11–7	Capt. R. Owen			20–1		
	Ilex	7–12–3	A. Nightingall			5–1		
1892	**Father O'Flynn**	7–10–5	Capt. R. Owen	Wilson	25	20–1	9.48⅕	g
	Cloister	8–12–3	Mr. J. C. Dormer			11–2		
	Ilex	8–12–7	A. Nightingall			20–1		
1893	**Cloister**	9–12–7	Dollery	Swatton	15	9–2f	9.32	f
	Aesop	a–10–4	H. Barker			100–12		
	Why Not	12–11–12	A. Nightingall			5–1		
1894	**Why Not**	13–11–3	A. Nightingall	Collins	14	5–1jf	9.45⅖	g
	Lady Ellen II	6–9–10	T. Kavanagh			25–1		
	Wild Man from Borneo	6–10–9	Mr. J. Widger			40–1		
1895	**Wild Man from Borneo**	7–10–11	Mr. J. Widger	Gatland	19	10–1	10.32	h
	Cathal	6–10–9	H. Escott			100–8		
	Van der Berg	a–9–13	Dollery			25–1		
1896	**The Soarer**	a–9–13	Mr. D. Campbell	Collins	28	40–1	10.11⅕	g
	Father O'Flynn	11–10–12	Mr. C. Grenfell			40–1		
	Biscuit	a–10–0	Mathews			25–1		

The Winners and Placed Horses, 1837–1970

Year	Result and Distances 1st. 2nd. 3rd.	Age & Weight	Rider	Trainer	Runners	S.P.	Time M.Secs.	Going
1897	**Manifesto**	9-11-3	T. Kavanagh	McAuliffe	28	6-1f	9.49	g
	Filbert	a-9-7	Mr. C. Beatty			100-1		
	Ford of Fyne	6-10-7	Mr. Withington			25-1		
1898	**Drogheda**	6-10-12	J. Gourley	E. Woods	24	25-1	9.43⁴⁄₅	h
	Cathal	a-11-5	Mr. R. Ward			7-1		
	Gauntlet	a-10-13	W. Taylor			100-12		
1899	**Manifesto**	11-12-7	G. Williamson	R. Collins	19	5-1	9.49⁴⁄₅	g
	Ford of Fyne	8-10-10	E. Mathews			40-1		
	Elliman	a-10-1	A. E. Piggott			20-1		
1900	**Ambush II**	6-11-3	A. Anthony	A. Anthony	16	4-1	10.1	g
	Barsac 4	a-9-12	W. Halsey			25-1		
	Manifesto Nk.	12-12-13	G. Williamson			6-1		
1901	**Grudon**	9-10-0	A. Nightingall	J. Holland	24	9-1	9.47⁴⁄₅	h
	Drumcree 4	7-9-12	Mr. H. Nugent			10-1		
	Buffalo Bill 6	a-9-7	H. Taylor			33-1		
1902	**Shannon Lass**	a-10-1	D. Reid	Hackett	21	20-1	10.3	h
	Mathew 3	6-9-12	W. Morgan			50-1		
	Manifesto 3	14-12-8	A. E. Piggott			100-6		
1903	**Drumcree**	9-11-3	P. Woodland	Sir C. Nugent	23	13-2f	10.0²⁄₅	g
	Detail 3	7-9-13	A. Nightingall			100-14		
	Manifesto 20	15-12-3	G. Williamson			25-1		
1904	**Moifaa**	8-10-7	A. Birch	O. Hickey	26	25-1	9.59	g
	Kirkland 8	8-10-10	F. Mason			100-7		
	The Gunner Nk.	7-10-4	Mr. J. Widger			25-1		
1905	**Kirkland**	9-11-5	F. Mason	Thomas	27	6-1	9.48¹⁄₅	g
	Napper Tandy 3	8-10-0	P. Woodland			25-1		
	Buckaway II 4	7-9-11	A. Newey			100-1		

The Winners and Placed Horses, 1837–1970   113

Year	Result and Distances 1st. 2nd. 3rd.	Age & Weight	Rider	Trainer	Runners	S.P.	Time M.Secs.	Going
1906	**Ascectic's Silver** Red Lad 10 Aunt May 2	9–10–9 6–10–2 a–11–2	Mr. A. Hastings C. Kelly Mr. H. Persse	A. Hastings	23	20–1 33–1 25–1	9.34⅕	g
1907	**Eremon** Tom West 6 Patlander Bad	7–10–1 8–9–12 11–10–7	A. Newey H. Murphy J. Lynn	T. Coulthwaite	23	8–1 100–6 50–1	9.47⅕	g
1908	**Rubio** Mattie Macgregor 10 The Lawyer III 6	a–10–5 6–10–6 a–10–13	H. Bletsoe W. Bissell Mr. P. Whittaker	W. Costello	24	66–1 25–1 100–7	10.33⅕	h
1909	**Lutteur III** Judas 2 Caubeen Bad	5–10–11 a–10–10 9–11–7	G. Parfrement R. Chadwick F. Mason	H. Escott	32	11–1f 33–1 20–1	9.53⅘	g
1910	**Jenkinstown** Jerry M 3 Odor 3	9–10–5 7–12–7 a–9–7	R. Chadwick E. Driscoll Mr. R. Hall	T. Coulthwaite	25	100–8 6–1 100–1	10.4⅘	g
1911	**Glenside** Rathnally 20 Shady Girl 3	9–10–3 6–11–0 a–10–5	Mr. J. Anthony R. Chadwick G. Clancy	Capt. Collis	26	20–1 8–1 33–1	10.4⅘	h
1912	**Jerry M** Bloodstone 6 Axle Pin 4	9–12–7 10–11–6 8–10–2	E. Piggott F. Lyall I. Anthony	R. Gore	24	4–1jf 40–1 20–1	10.13⅖	g
1913	**Covercoat** Irish Mail Dist. Carsey Dist.	7–11–6 6–11–4 10–12–0	P. Woodland Mr. O. Anthony Mr. H. Drake	R. Gore	23	100–9 25–1 100–9	10.19	g
1914	**Sunloch** Trianon III 8 Lutteur III 8	8–9–7 9–11–9 10–12–6	W. J. Smith C. Hawkins A. Carter	T. Tyler	20	100–6 100–8 10–1	9.58⅘	g

Year	Result and Distances 1st. 2nd. 3rd.	Age & Weight	Rider	Trainer	Runners	S.P.	Time M.Secs.	Going
1915	**Ally Sloaper**	6-10-6	Mr. J. Anthony	A. Hastings	20	100-8	9.47$\frac{4}{5}$	g
	Jacobus 2	8-11-0	A. Newey			25-1		
	Father Confessor 8	6-9-10	A. Aylin			10-1		

1916, 1917, and 1918 Substitute Race at Gatwick

Year	Result and Distances 1st. 2nd. 3rd.	Age & Weight	Rider	Trainer	Runners	S.P.	Time M.Secs.	Going
1919	**Poethlyn**	9-12-7	E. Piggott	H. E. Escott	22	11-4f	10.8$\frac{2}{5}$	g
	Ballyboggan 8	8-11-10	W. Head			9-1		
	Pollen 6	10-11-4	A. Escott			100-7		
1920	**Troytown**	7-11-9	Mr. J. Anthony	A. Anthony	24	6-1	10.20$\frac{1}{5}$	h
	The Turk II 12	10-9-7	R. Burford			—		
	The Bore 6	9-10-1	Mr. H. Brown			28-1		
1921	**Shaun Spadah**	10-11-7	F. Rees	G. C. Poole	35	100-9	10.26	h
	The Bore Dist.	10-11-8	Mr. H. Brown			9-1		
	All White Dist.	7-10-13	R. Chadwick			33-1		
1922	**Music Hall**	9-11-8	L. Rees	O. Anthony	32	100-9	9.55$\frac{4}{5}$	g
	Drifter 12	8-10-0	Watkinson			18-1		
	Taffytus 6	9-11-0	T. Leader			66-1		
1923	**Sergeant Murphy**	13-11-3	Capt. G. Bennett	G. Blackwell	28	100-6	9.36	g
	Shaun Spadah 3	12-12-7	F. Rees			20-1		
	Conjuror II 6	11-11-0	Mr. C. Dewhurst			100-6		
1924	**Master Robert**	11-10-5	R. Trudgill	A. Hastings	30	25-1	9.40	g
	Fly Mask 4	10-10-12	J. Moylan			100-7		
	Silvo 6	8-12-2	G. Goswell			100-7		
1925	**Double Chance**	9-10-9	Maj. J. P. Wilson	F. Archer	33	100-9	9.42$\frac{3}{5}$	g
	Old Tay Bridge 4	11-11-12	J. Anthony			9-1		
	Fly Mask 6	11-11-11	E. C. Doyle			10-1		

The Winners and Placed Horses, 1837–1970 115

Year	Result and Distances 1st. 2nd. 3rd.	Age & Weight	Rider	Trainer	Runners	S.P.	Time M.Secs.	Going
1926	**Jack Horner**	9–10–5	W. Watkinson	H. Leader	30	25–1	9.36	g
	Old Tay Bridge 3	12–12–2	J. Anthony			8–1		
	Bright's Boy 1	7–11–8	E. Doyle			25–1		
1927	**Sprig**	10–12–4	T. E. Leader	T. R. Leader	37	8–1f	10.20⅕	h
	Bovril III 1	9–10–12	Mr. G. W. Pennington			100–1		
	Bright's Boy 1	8–12–7	J. Anthony			100–7		
1928	**Tipperary Tim**	10–10–0	W. P. Dutton	J. Dodd	42	100–1	10.23⅖	h
	Billy Barton Dist.	10–10–11	T. Cullinan			33–1		
	Only two finished							
1929	**Gregalach**	7–11–4	R. Everett	T. R. Leader	66	100–1	9.47⅖	g
	Easter Hero 6	9–12–7	J. Moloney			9–2		
	Richmond II Bad	6–10–5	W. Stott			40–1		
1930	**Shaun Goilin**	10–11–7	T. Cullinan	F. Hartigan	41	100–8	9.40⅗	g
	Melleray's Belle Nk.	11–10–0	J. Mason			20–1		
	Sir Lindsay 1½	9–10–6	D. Williams			100–7		
1931	**Grakle**	9–11–7	R. Lyall	T. Coulthwaite	43	100–6	9.32⅘	g
	Gregalach 1½	9–12–0	J. Moloney			25–1		
	Annandale 10	9–10–7	T. Morgan			100–1		
1932	**Forbra**	7–10–7	J. Hamey	T. R. Rimell	36	50–1	9.44⅗	g
	Egremont 3	8–10–7	Mr. E. C. Paget			33–1		
	Shaun Goilin Bad	12–12–4	D. Williams			40–1		
1933	**Kellsboro' Jack**	7–11–9	D. Williams	I. Anthony	34	25–1	9.28	g/f
	Really True 3	a–10–12	Mr. F. Furlong			66–1		
	Slater Nk.	a–10–7	Mr. M. Barry			50–1		
1934	**Golden Miller**	7–12–2	G. Wilson	B. Briscoe	30	8–1	9.20⅖	g/f
	Delaneige 5	a–11–6	J. Moloney			100–7		
	Thomond II 5	a–12–4	W. Speck			18–1		

The Winners and Placed Horses, 1837–1970

Year	Result and Distances 1st. 2nd. 3rd.	Age & Weight	Rider	Trainer	Runners	S.P.	Time M.Secs.	Going
1935	**Reynoldstown**	8-11-4	Mr. F. Furlong	Maj. F. Furlong	27	22-1	9.21	g/f
	Blue Prince 3	a-10-7	W. Parvin			40-1		
	Thomond II 8	a-11-13	W. Speck			9-2		
1936	**Reynoldstown**	9-12-2	Mr. F. Walwyn	Maj. F. Furlong	35	10-1	9.37	g
	Ego 12	a-10-8	Mr. H. Llewellyn			50-1		
	Bachelor Prince 6	a-10-9	J. Fawcus			66-1		
1937	**Royal Mail**	8-11-13	E. Williams	I. Anthony	33	100-6	9.59$\frac{3}{5}$	s
	Cooleen 3	9-11-4	J. Fawcus			33-1		
	Pucka Belle 10	11-10-7	Mr. E. Bailey			100-6		
1938	**Battleship**	11-11-6	B. Hobbs	R. Hobbs	36	40-1	9.29$\frac{4}{5}$	g/f
	Royal Danieli Hd.	7-11-3	D. Moore			18-1		
	Workman Bad	8-10-2	J. Brogan			28-1		
1939	**Workman**	9-10-6	T. Hyde	Ruttle	37	100-8	9.42$\frac{1}{5}$	g
	MacMoffat 3	7-10-3	I. Alder			25-1		
	Kilstar 15	8-10-3	G. Archibald			8-1		
1940	**Bogskar**	7-10-4	M. Jones	Lord Stalbridge	30	25-1	9.20$\frac{3}{5}$	g/f
	MacMoffat 4	8-10-10	I. Alder			8-1		
	Gold Arrow 6	8-10-3	P. Lay			50-1		

1941–1945   NO RACE

1946	**Lovely Cottage**	9-10-8	Capt. R. Petre	T. Rayson	34	25-1	9.38$\frac{1}{5}$	g
	Jack Finlay 4	7-10-2	W. Kidney			100-1		
	Prince Regent 3	11-12-5	T. Hyde			3-1		
1947	**Caughoo**	8-10-0	E. Dempsey	McDowell	57	100-1	10.3$\frac{4}{5}$	h
	Lough Conn 20	11-10-1	D. McCann			33-1		
	Kami 4	10-10-13	Mr. J. Hislop			33-1		

Year	Result and Distances 1st. 2nd. 3rd.	Age & Weight	Rider	Trainer	Runners	S.P.	Time M.Secs.	Going
1948	**Sheila's Cottage** First of the Dandies 1 Cromwell 6	9–10–7 11–10–4 7–10–11	A. P. Thompson J. Brogan Lord Mildmay	N. Crump	43	50–1 25–1 33–1	9.25$\frac{2}{5}$	g/f
1949	**Russian Hero** Roimond 8 Royal Mount 1	9–10–8 8–11–12 10–10–12	L. McMorrow R. Francis P. Doyle	G. Owen	43	66–1 22–1 18–1	9.24$\frac{1}{5}$	g/f
1950	**Freebooter** Wot No Sun 15 Acthon Major 10	9–11–11 8–11–8 10–11–2	J. Power A. P. Thompson R. O'Ryan	R. Renton	49	10–1 100–7 33–1	9.23$\frac{3}{5}$	g/f
1951	**Nickel Coin** Royal Tan 6 Derrinstown Bad	9–10–1 7–10–13 11–10–0	J. Bullock Mr. A. O'Brien A. Power	J. O'Donoghue	36	40–1 22–1 66–1	9.48$\frac{4}{5}$	s
1952	**Teal** Legal Joy 5 Wot No Sun Bad	10–10–12 9–10–4 10–11–7	A. P. Thompson M. Scudamore D. V. Dick	N. Crump	47	100–7 100–6 33–1	9.21	g/f
1953	**Early Mist** Mont Tremblant 20 Irish Lizard 4	8–11–2 7–12–5 10–10–6	B. Marshall D. V. Dick R. Turnell	M. V. O'Brien	31	20–1 18–1 33–1	9.22$\frac{4}{5}$	g
1954	**Royal Tan** Tudor Line Nk. Irish Lizard 10	10–11–7 9–10–7 11–10–5	B. Marshall G. Slack M. Scudamore	M. V. O'Brien	29	8–1 10–1 15–2	9.32$\frac{4}{5}$	s
1955	**Quare Times** Tudor Line 12 Carey's Cottage 4	9–11–0 10–11–3 8–10–11	P. Taaffe G. Slack T. Taaffe	M. V. O'Brien	30	100–9 10–1 20–1	10.19$\frac{1}{5}$	h
1956	**E.S.B.** Gentle Moya 10 Royal Tan 10	10–11–3 10–10–2 12–12–1	D. Dick G. Milburn T. Taaffe	T. F. Rimell	29	100–7 22–1 28–1	9.21$\frac{2}{5}$	g

The Winners and Placed Horses, 1837–1970

Year	Result and Distances 1st. 2nd. 3rd.	Age & Weight	Rider	Trainer	Runners	S.P.	Time M.Secs.	Going
1957	**Sundew**	11–11–7	F. Winter	F. Hudson	35	20–1	9.42⅗	g/s
	Wyndburgh 8	7–10–7	M. Batchelor			25–1		
	Tiberetta 6	9–10–0	A. Oughton			66–1		
1958	**Mr. What**	8–10–6	A. Freeman	T. Taaffe	31	18–1	9.59⅘	h
	Tiberetta 30	10–10–6	G. Slack			28–1		
	Green Drill 15	8–10–10	G. Milburn			28–1		
1959	**Oxo**	8–10–13	M. Scudamore	W. Stephenson	34	8–1	9.37⅘	g
	Wyndburgh 1½	8–10–13	T. Brookshaw			10–1		
	Mr. What 8	9–11–9	T. Taaffe			6–1		
1960	**Merryman II**	9–10–12	G. Scott	N. Crump	26	13–2	9.27	g
	Badanloch 15	9–10–9	S. Mellor			100–7		
	Clear Profit 12	10–10–1	B. Wilkinson			20–1		
1961	**Nicolaus Silver**	9–10–1	H. Beasley	T. F. Rimell	35	28–1	9.22⅗	f
	Merryman II 5	10–11–12	D. Ancil			8–1		
	O'Malley Point Nk.	10–11–4	P. Farrell			100–6		
1962	**Kilmore**	12–10–4	F. Winter	H. R. Price	32	28–1	9.50	h
	Wyndburgh 10	12–10–9	T. Barnes			45–1		
	Mr. What 10	12–10–0	J. Lehane			22–1		
1963	**Ayala**	9–10–0	P. Buckley	K. Piggott	47	66–1	9.35⅘	s
	Carrickbeg ¾	7–10–3	Mr. J. Lawrence			20–1		
	Hawa's Song 5	10–10–0	P. Broderick			28–1		
1964	**Team Spirit**	12–10–3	G. W. Robinson	F. Walwyn	33	18–1	9.47	s
	Purple Silk ½	9–10–4	J. Kenneally			100–6		
	Peacetown 6	10–10–1	R. Edwards			40–1		
1965	**Jay Trump**	8–11–5	Mr. T. Smith, Junr.	F. Winter	47	100–6	9.30⅗	g
	Freddie ¾	8–11–10	P. McCarron			7–2		
	Mr. Jones 20	9–11–5	Mr. C. Collins			50–1		

The Winners and Placed Horses, 1837–1970

Year	Result and Distances 1st. 2nd. 3rd.	Age & Weight	Rider	Trainer	Runners	S.P.	Time M.Secs.	Going
1966	**Anglo**	8–10–0	T. Norman	F. Winter	47	50–1	9.52 4/5	g
	Freddie 3/4	9–11–7	P. McCarron			11–4		
	Forest Prince 20	8–10–8	G. Scott			100–7		
1967	**Foinavon**	9–10–0	J. Buckingham	J. Kempton	44	100–1	9.49 3/5	g
	Honey End 15	10–10–4	J. Gifford			15–2		
	Red Alligator 3	8–10–0	B. Fletcher			30–1		
1968	**Red Alligator**	9–10–0	B. Fletcher	Denys Smith	45	100–7	9.28 4/5	g
	Moidore's Token 20	11–10–8	B. Brogan			100–6		
	Different Class Nk.	8–11–5	D. Mould			17–2		
1969	**Highland Wedding**	12–10–4	E. P. Harty	G. Balding	30	100–9	9.30 4/5	g
	Steel Bridge 12	11–10–0	R. Pitman			50–1		
	Rondetto 1	13–10–6	J. King			25–1		
1970	**Gay Trip**	8–11–5	P. Taaffe	T. F. Rimell	28	15–1	9.38	g/f
	Vulture 20	8–10–0	S. Barker			15–1		
	Miss Hunter 1/2	9–10–0	F. Shortt			33–1		
1971	**Specify**	9–10–13	J. Cook	J. Sutcliffe	38	28–1	9.33 4/5	g/f
	Black Secret Nk.	7–11–5	Mr. J. Dreaper			20–1		
	Astbury 2	8–10–0	J. Bourke			33–1		

Abbreviations: h = heavy   s = soft   g/s = good to soft   g = good   g/f = good to firm   f = firm.

Index

Abd-el-Kader, 22, 26, 75
Aesop, 77
Airlie, Lord, 70
Alcibiade, 27
Amberwave, 38, 56
Ambush II, 25, 78, 79, 82
Anatis, 26
Anglo, 25, 30
Anthony, Mr. J, 29, 50, 85, 86
Arbury, 25, 92
Archer, Fred, 72
Archer, Frederick, 72
Arkle, 20, 100, 101
Ascetic, 25, 78
Ascetic's Silver, 18, 27, 78
Assheton-Smith, Sir Charles, 83
Austerlitz, 25, 91
Auteuil, 86
Avenger, 18
Axle Pin, 84
Ayala, 49

Barsac, 78, 79, 82
Battleship, 22, 24, 25, 29, 49, 86
B.B.C., 98
Beasley, Mr. H, 76
Beasley, Mr. T., 29, 60, 61
Becher, Capt., 7
Becher 'Chase, The, 90
Benson & Hedges Gold Cup, 101
Bicester, Lord, 33, 90
Billy Barton, 44
Bloodstone, 84
Bogskar, 25
Bore, The, 86
Bottomley, Mr. H., 79
Boyce, Charles, 58, 92
Boyle, Leonard, 91
Bright's Boy, 44
Brookshaw, Tim, 92
Brown, Mr. Harry, 92
Buckley, Pat, 49
Bulteel, Mr., 79

Carrickbeg, 49
Carter, Alec, 41
Casse Tete, 26
Cathal, 79
Caughoo, 37
Champion 'Chase, The, 86, 87, 90, 92
Chandler, 66
Cheltenham Gold Cup, The, 86, 87, 100, 101, 102
Churchtown, 50
Cloncarrig, 90, 91
Cloister, 24, 26, 27, 41, 50, 76–78
Collins-Gerrard, Maj., 86
Colonel, The, 24, 26, 42, 75, 91
Come Away, 76
Conney burrow, 50
Cortolvin, 45, 52
Cottage, 25
Cottage Welcome, 90
Covercoat, 84
Covert Hack, 82

Cromwell, 90
Crump, Capt. N., 29
Cundell, Frank, 70
Cushalu Mavourneen, 29
Cyrus, 29, 60, 61, 66

Davy Jones, 42
Delaneige, 87
Delarue, 33
de Rothschild, Mr. A., 72
Despatch, 70
Devon Loch, 52, 54, 94
Dick, Dave, 33, 52
Distance Judge, 12
Disturbance, 25, 60, 75, 91
Double Chance, 52, 72
Douglas-Pennant, Maj., 70
Drumcree, 29, 78
Drumree, 29
Duff, Mr. C., 77, 83
Dutton, Mr, W. P., 44
Dyas, Mr. H., 79

Early Mist, 86
Easter Hero, 56
Ede, Mr. George, 35
"Edwards Mr.," 35
Eider 'Chase, The, 102
Elizabeth, Queen, The Queen Mother, 52
Elmore, John, 74
Emblem, 25, 26
Emblematic, 25, 26
Emigrant, 58, 75, 92
Empress, 25, 26, 29, 60, 75, 91
Eremon, 52, 91
E.S.B., 52, 54, 66, 86

Fan, 45
Father O'Flynn, 76
Filbert, 79
First of the Dandies, 46
Fly Mask, 52, 72
Foinavon, 24, 56
Foolhardy, 37
Forbra, 87
Ford of Fyne, 79, 82
Francis, Dick, 52, 54
Freddie, 27, 92
Freebooter, 26, 86, 90–91
Free Trader, 25, 26, 27
Frigate, 26, 27, 75

Gamecock, 91
Gentle Ida, 79
Glenside, 29, 37, 84
Golden Miller, 18, 26, 30, 33, 38, 54, 86–90, 100
Goodman, Mr. A., 29
Gore, Bob, 83, 84
Grace II, 78
Grakle, 28, 44, 86
Grand Annual Steeplechase, The, 91
Grand Liverpool Steeplechase, The, 3
Grand Prix de Paris, 86
Grand Sefton Steeplechase, The, 77, 78, 90
Great Shropshire Steeplechase, The, 77
Great Spann, 44

Green C., 29
Green, Mr. S., 70
Gregalach, 23, 86
Grudon, 35, 37
Gubbins, Mr. J., 60

Half Caste, 25
Hastings, Aubrey, 70
Hawkins, Charles, 41
Heartbreak Hill, 46
Hennessey Gold Cup, The, 101
Hidden Mystery, 82
Hislop, John, 14
Hobbs, Bruce, 29
Hodgman, Mr., 58
Hornihiharriho, 29
Horse Race Betting Levy Board, 16, 98
Hyde, Tim, 56

Ilex, 22, 24, 91
Irish Hospital Sweepstake, 98
Irish Lizard, 27, 50, 92

Jackdaw, 25
Jarvis, Sir Jack, 92
Jay Trump, 27, 86
Jealousy, 26
Jenkinstown, 29
Jerry M, 26, 79, 83–5
Jewitt, James, 60
Jockey Club, The, 7, 102

Kellsboro' Jack, 37, 86
Kendal, 91
KGB, 33
Kinsky, Count, 32
Kirkland, 78
Knight of Gwynne, The, 27, 92
Kohn, Mrs. G., 66

Lady Grundrose, 77
Lamb, The, 22, 24, 26, 35, 70, 75
Lambton, The Hon. Geo., 18, 74, 101
Lancashire 'Chase, The, 91
Land, Ben, 58
Lawrence, John, 49
Beach, Jack, 30
Liberator, 75
Linde, Henry, 17, 29, 58, 60, 77
Little, Capt. J., 70
Liverpool Foxhunters' Chase, The, 104
Lottery, 7, 22, 74, 91
Lovely Cottage, 29, 56
Lutteur III, 18, 25, 41

Machell, Capt., 60, 61, 66
MacMoffat, 92
Maguelonne, 44
Manifesto, 26, 78–83, 90, 92, 102
Manners, Lord, 58, 60, 61
Marsh, Richard, 76
Marshall, Bryan, 29, 32, 50
Mason, Finch, 3
Mason, Jem, 75
Master Robert, 70, 72
McAuliffe, Willie, 79
McDonough, Alan, 75
McKinley, Mr. R., 70
Merryman II, 98, 102

Mildmay, Lord, 42, 90
Mill House, 20
Miss Mowbray, 26, 27
Mr. What, 29, 91
Mohican, 60
Moifaa, 18, 22, 50, 78
Molony, Jack, 33
Monaveen, 90
Mum, 79
Music Hall, 23, 86
My Prince, 25

National Hunt Committee, The, 1
New Century Steeplechase, The, 84
Newey, Alfred, 52, 92
Nickel Coin, 26
Nicolaus Silver, 24
Nightingall, A., 22, 24, 27

O'Brien, Vincent, 29
Old Tay Bridge, 52
Oliver, Tom, 27
Out and About, 39
Owen, Capt. Roddy, 76

Page, J., 29
Paget, Miss D., 90, 100
Paris Steeplechase, The, 84
Pathfinder, 27, 29
Payne, Bill, 44
Peel, Capt., 66
Permit, 101
Peter Simple, 26, 75, 92
Petre, Capt. R., 56
Pickernell, Mr. T., 27, 35
Piggott, Ernest, 29
Pioneer, 25, 29
Pistache, 79
Poethyln, 26, 86
Poulet, Lord, 35
Power, Jimmy, 90
Power, Mr., 9
Prince of Wales, H.R.H., 79
Prince Regent, 20, 56, 102
Prix des Drags, 86
Purple Silk, 49

Quare Times, 29

Racing Calendar, The, 102
Rathnally, 37
Reavey, Eddie, 46
Red Alligator, 25
Red Prince II, 91
Regal, 24, 60
Reugny, 25, 60, 91
Reynoldstown, 18, 24, 26, 29, 42, 86, 90
Richardson, Mr. J. M., 29, 32
Rimmell, T. F., 29
Roimond, 90
Royal Danieli, 49
Royal Mail, 24, 86
Royal Tan, 50, 86
Rubio, 70
Russian Hero, 90

Salamander, 52, 70, 75, 91
Schweppes, Messrs, 98
Scott, The, 60

Scottish Grand National, 101
Seaman, 29, 60, 61
Sefton, Lord, 12
Sergeant Murphy, 86
Seventy-Four, 27, 92
Shady Girl, 37
Shannon Lass, 26, 78
Shaun Goilin, 28, 86
Shaun Spadah, 18, 86
Sheila's Cottage, 26, 29
Sherriff Hutton, 79
Shifnal, 25
Silvo, 72
Sir John, 92
Skouras, 90
Smith, W. J., 41
Soarer, The, 79
Sprig, 26, 44, 86
Stanley 'Chase, The, 84, 86
Steel Point, 90
Stevens, George, 27, 29
Studd, Mr. E., 70
Sundew, 66, 86
Sunloch, 41

Taaffe, Pat, 29
Taaffe, Toss, 50
Teal, 50, 90
Team Spirit, 27, 49
"Thomas, Mr.," 27, 29, 35
Thomond II, 87
Thompson, A., 29, 32
Thompson, Mr. C., 77
Tiberetta, 92
Timon, 79
Tipperary Tim, 44, 91
Tophams, Messrs, 16
Trianon III, 41
Troytown, 29, 41, 50, 85–6
Trudgill, Bob, 72
Tudor Line, 50, 92
Turk II, 86

Valentine, 9
Valentine 'Chase, The, 78
Vanguard, 25
Vigors, T., 79
Voluptuary, 27, 91
Vulgan, 25

Wanderer, 25
Weathercock, 58, 92
Welsh Grand National, The, 77
Westminster, 58
Weatherbys, Messrs, 77
Whitbread Gold Cup, The, 101
Why Not, 24
Wild Man from Borneo, The, 78, 79
Williamson, George, 82
Wilson, Mr. E., 29
Wilson, Gerry, 33
Winter, Fred, 29, 66
Woodbrook, 29, 60
Woodland, P., 29
Workman, 49
Wyndburgh, 27, 92

Xanthus, 92

Zarter, 90
Zoedone, 26, 32